Dollars® for Scholars

The Autobiography of
Dr. Irving A. Fradkin
Founder of Citizens' Scholarship
Foundation of America, Inc.

with Michael J. Vieira

BRANDEN PUBLISHING COMPANY
Boston

Library of Congress Cataloging-in-Publication Data

Fradkin, Irving A., 1921-
Dollars for scholars : the autobiography of Dr. Irving A. Fradkin, founder of Citizens' Scholarship Foundation of America, Inc. / with Michael J. Vieira.
p.cm.
Includes bibliographical references and index.
ISBN 0-8283-1974-X (first edition)
ISBN 0-8283- 2080-2 $17.95 (second edition)

1. Citizens' Scholarship Foundation of AmericaHistory.
2. Fradkin, Irving A., 1921- .
3. BenefactorsUnited StatesBiography.
I. Vieira, Michael J.II. Title.
LB2338.F731993
371.2'3'0973dc20 93-26042
CIP

B|B

Branden Books
Division of Branden Publishing Company, Inc.
P.O. Box 812094
Wellesley MA 02482

FOREWORD

This edition of "Dollars for Scholars" is an updated report on the progress and success of the first grassroots scholarship movement in the United States, and one of the major programs of Citizens' Scholarship Foundation of America℠ (CSFA), the nation's largest private sector scholarship and educational support organization. The tremendous growth of CSFA continues, and new programs have been introduced and developed to help further the success of its Dollars for Scholars® program and its chapters.

Please note the additions to this book concerning ScholarShop® and the American Dream Challenge, both designed to reach youth at earlier ages and show them the critical importance of education in their lives. Citizens' Scholarship Foundation of America's Scholarship Management Services™ program also continues to grow and reaches thousands of additional students every year. A chapter has also been added about the Families of Freedom Scholarship Fund® created by CSFA to provide educational assistance to financially needy dependents of the September 11 terrorist attacks and the ensuing rescue efforts.

I've been overwhelmed by the exemplary and dedicated people who have helped to make CSFA the nation's largest private sector scholarship and educational support organization.

Since 1986, we have been under the superb and inspired leadership of Dr. William C. Nelsen, who has further built this organization as a positive force in America. Under his direction, as of July, 2002, CSFA has increased the number of Dollars for Scholars chapters from 200 to more than 1,100 in 39 states and the District of Columbia. It has increased its number of Scholarship Management Services clients, which include corporations, foundations and others, from 200 to more than 900. It has established its ScholarShop program in 172 communities. And it has attracted 445 postsecondary institutions to the Collegiate Partners program.

Since CSFA was founded in 1958, it has distributed, through its three programs, over $911.5 million to nearly 850,000 students. In 2001 alone, CSFA programs reported or committed a record total of over $135.3 million in assistance to more than 101,145 students.

This amazing success story demonstrates what people in a free society can do when they work together.

The original edition of this book appeared in 1993. And now, eight years later, we have shown conclusively that our half-million scholarship recipients have gone on to become leaders in their communities—teachers, administrators, health and business professionals, and in countless other occupations. The students CSFA has supported have given back to help make a better America.

–Dr. Irving Fradkin

A SPECIAL DEDICATION

In memory of the late beloved Sam Levenson, the foremost humorist and humanitarian of his time. He was installed as the first and only Honorary President of Citizens' Scholarship Foundation of America on January 11, 1961. He declared, "I expect this scholarship program to become one of our great national projects, supported by every citizen in every hamlet of America."

CONTENTS

"Ask not what this country can do for you,
but what you can do for your country."
—*John F. Kennedy*

INTRODUCTION

by Michael J. Vieira

From President John F. Kennedy urging Americans to "ask what you can do for your country" to President George Bush recognizing "a thousand points of light," to President Clinton calling for "sacrifice" and "national service," government leaders have tried to encourage a spirit of volunteerism and commitment in all Americans. Few have taken it to heart like Dr. Irving A. Fradkin.

As a free-lance writer, I first met Dr. Fradkin when he suggested that I cover a Citizens' Scholarship Foundation of America^{SM} (CSFA) program. Although the event was interesting, I was more curious about meeting the man who had become somewhat of a legend in my home town of Fall River, Massachusetts.

During an interview, the soft-spoken gentleman wove his tale of how he founded Citizens' Scholarship Foundation of America in 1958 as part of his unsuccessful attempt at running for School Committee. While many politicians forget their pledges soon after the election results come in, Dr. Fradkin, despite his defeat, not only kept his promise, but has helped CSFA spread across the country, aiding thousands of young people with millions of dollars.

At the time, I found the story more than interesting; it was just a little incredible. Other programs had collected dollars before and other scholarship plans had worked, but I knew of no other project that had grown from one community to a region to a national grass roots movement just on the wave of enthusiasm by a group of people committed to helping others.

Normally, Dr. Fradkin doesn't like to talk about himself or his part in developing CSFA. He would rather share his vision for America and focus on the role others have had in making the Foundation one of the most successful in the history of this country.

At the urging of many, he is finally now willing to tell his story and share his vision a vision which is rooted in education and nourished by the communities which provide their own youth with, as Dr. Fradkin often says, "a hand up not a hand out." His America is one where race, religion, color and sex are part of the kaleidoscope, which makes this country unique and beautiful, not which separate and divide.

His view of America is also realistic, acknowledging that we have one of the highest crime rates and lowest literacy rates in the western world. Dr. Fradkin points to the media's preoccupation with sex and violence as a symptom of a nation in serious trouble, and cites figures from historian Arnold Toynbee, which show that of 21 civilizations, 19 have died from decay within.

He frequently pulls from his wallet a piece of paper, which contains historian Edward Gibbon's reasons why the Roman Empire fell. They read:

"1. The undermining of the dignity and sanctity of the home, which is the basis for human society.

"2. Higher and higher taxes: the spending of public money for free bread and circuses for the populace.

"3. The mad craze for pleasure, with sports and plays becoming more exciting, more brutal and more immoral.

"4. The building of great armaments when the real enemy was within the decay of individual responsibility.

"5. The decay of religion, whose leaders lost touch with life and their power to guide."

He makes his point. America is in trouble.

Dr. Fradkin is not pessimistic, however. He also tells positive tales of the welfare mothers who have returned to school thanks to help from their local Citizens' Scholarship Foundation "Dollars for Scholars" chapter, of communities separated by prejudice and fear

Like many others who have been touched by the man, I have come to believe that America can be made better and that CSFA is a tool which will provide example and experience to those interested in improving democracy. Dr. Fradkin wants you to believe again, as well, which is why this book has been written.

As Dr. Fradkin has said:

"The purpose and dream of CSFA is to motivate and inspire our future leaders to give something of themselves back to their communities and their country, so that they can better understand and appreciate the dream of democracy and perpetuate our priceless freedom ... to bring about a better, more peaceful and more productive America."

While the story begins with Dr. Fradkin, it revolves around the amazing grass roots success of CSFA, which started with $500 in 1961 and has awarded almost $911.5 million in assistance to nearly 850,000 young people since it began.

Although the numbers are impressive, Dr. Fradkin won't be satisfied until every community in every state has adopted CSFA—because he believes not only that educated young people are the answer to building a better America, but also that the very process of working together is an exercise in democracy and the ability to help another person in need is the responsibility that goes with our priceless freedom.

That's the real story about to be told. It's the story of a retired optometrist who feels he has everything democracy can provide: a successful marriage, three children and three grandchildren, and enough money to be satisfied and to provide for his family.

"Money is not my God," he often says, adding that he has everything good that America has to offer.

But he's not completely satisfied. What he really wants is to leave his children and grandchildren and your children and grandchildren a better America.

While the story of the man is inspiring, so too are the results of Citizens' Scholarship Foundation of America. It's the tale of a program, which has worked in many communities, for many corporations, with many colleges and is still growing.

It's also the answer to John F. Kennedy's question. What can you do for your country? We can work together to educate young people so that everyone can share in Dr. Fradkin's vision for America.

"We're in a war, but it's a winnable war, because of our youth. If we set the right example, if we provide discipline and support, if we challenge them, our young people — from even the most impoverished backgrounds — can compete with anyone in the world."

—John Pepper, President
Proctor & Gamble Company

PREFACE

If a caring person were to have a dialogue with God, he might ask:

"God, why do you allow such a terrible world so full of hate and crime, so torn by violence and bigotry? What are you going to do about it?"

"I created you, didn't I?" God might reply, "You're on earth. You have to be my ears and hands, my eyes and heart. It's up to you, working with me, to make a better world."

I love the idea of such a dialogue because it really shows that any individual can make a difference and because it symbolizes so well the work of Citizens' Scholarship Foundation of America. Looking back over the past decades to the beginning of CSFA and even further to the example of my parents, that theme has been repeated throughout my life: One person has the potential to make a difference.

I've always felt that there's more to life than just existing and making money. The most important thing a person can do is leave this world a better place than he or she found it.

Right from the start, that has been the whole premise of CSFA — each person has a God-given ability, a God-given gift which he or she can use to change this country and make it a better place in which to live.

Citizens' Scholarship Foundation of America offers more than financial aid. It provides the tools to give hope and opportunity to this country's young people. I firmly believe that the minds of the young people and their input into our country, not the gold and oil in the ground, will sustain the future of this country.

people and their input into our country, not the gold and oil in the ground, will sustain the future of this country.

If the minds and hearts of the future leaders can be motivated and inspired not just to develop their God-given abilities to the utmost, but to give something back, then CSFA is a success.

I am often asked, "Why do you bother spending so much time and energy traveling and speaking about CSFA and democracy?" I say, "Why not? I have all the advantages that this country can offer anybody."

I feel I have fulfilled the dream of democracy. But I believe that many Americans have lost sight of what our nation is and can be. If my story and this program can help them strive for that dream, then I will be happy.

This is the best country that has ever been, but there's no guarantee that it will last forever. To keep the dream alive, Americans have to get back to one basic idea: accepting responsibility for each other and for democracy.

Citizens' Scholarship Foundation started with the idea of helping one community, Fall River, Massachusetts, to help itself. But soon the idea germinated and grew, spreading across Massachusetts, throughout Rhode Island, and eventually across this country to many communities, colleges, and corporations.

Since our rather humble beginnings in Fall River, more than 1,100 local chapters, 445 colleges, and over 900 corporations of all sizes have adopted CSFA as their own.

In fact, there are many communities where CSFA's presence means no one is denied an education. Whether they are young people graduating from high school or older workers who need re-training, all students in need are helped by Citizens' Scholarship Foundation of America.

The money awarded, however, is just a commodity. More important are the examples and the experiences of people helping people.

In community after community, I have heard people say to CSFA organizers, "Thank you," but it hasn't just been the scholarship recipients who have been appreciative. The citizens in each city and town are grateful to the program for giving them dignity and the means to help their young. By working together, people get the feeling that they are doing something worthwhile, that they can be a force to build a community, and that they have been given a purpose in life.

Citizens' Scholarship Foundation is a prime example of an American success story. It proves that free people can do anything if given inspiration and ideas.

CSFA can work in every single community regardless of size. Communities who adopt the CSFA idea can change the lives of future leaders by giving them the training necessary to become more productive and the inspiration to become better citizens.

Unless young people take advantage of this country's excellent educational opportunities, they will be a detriment to themselves, to their families and to their society. They will be the last hired and the first fired.

According to the National Education Association, an estimated $260 billion each year is spent on students who drop out of school. What a shame, they have so many capabilities! So many times, all they need is hope and opportunity, and, of course, money too.

John F. Kennedy was an average student. Winston Churchill was an average student. Albert Einstein was almost thrown out of school. But they were motivated, and look at what they gave to this country and the world.

Citizens' Scholarship Foundation of America is still a grass roots program based on the idea that each person can make a difference by helping another person. Across this country, thousands of people have done just that. My story is just one example of a man who has touched others and has been touched by many — thanks to CSFA.

I believe in the dream of America. I believe that Americans, when properly motivated and inspired, are willing to assume leadership and responsibility to provide the higher education, skills, and knowledge needed to perpetuate our form of government — for the most valued and priceless asset our country possesses — our young people.

These young people will receive not only financial assistance, but a concrete and positive example — the example of their community willing to sacrifice to help them without regard to their race, religion, creed or color.

Dr. Barnaby Keeney, past president of Brown University, said, "The young people are less apt to hate and more apt to love and understand their neighbors when they see people of all nationalities, races, and colors willing to help them."

If our young people learn from this example of brotherhood in action instead of hearing mere words, won't they be more likely to carry the lesson all through life? That is my dream — that is the dream of Citizens' Scholarship Foundation of America. Once our young people learn how democracy truly works, then we can keep the American dream alive for our children and their children.

ACKNOWLEDGEMENTS

Without the love, support and assistance of Charlotte, my wife of 55 years, I would not have had the courage, fortitude and persistence to write and develop this history.

Thanks to my three wonderful children, Marlene, Bob, and Russ, daughters-in-law Jane and Goedele, and grandchildren Jeff, Karen and Jessica for their critiques, encouragement and concern.

Special thanks also go to:

Isabelle Cabral, my office receptionist for 49 years, for listening to my dreams and frustrations over the years, as well as for her encouragement.

The *Fall River Herald News* for the many editorials, feature stories and news items, which helped to spread the CSF concept throughout the area and the country.

Our CSFA president and my valued friend, Dr. William C. Nelsen, for his encouragement, inspiring chapter on the future of CSFA, and for his constructive criticism and ideas.

The Honor Roll Trustees of CSFA for their support and encouragement of this book.

Pat Samples, for her detailed and caring editorial critique and revisions of the manuscript.

Terri Kirby, for her careful work in word processing and reworking of the final manuscript.

Michael J. Vieira, my friend and collaborator, whose literary ability, patience and interest have made this book possible. He has taken my scrapbooks, tapes and notes and put them together into a readable book.

Thanks also to Mike's wife, Audrey; his children, Anne and Jonathan; and the publications' staffs at B.M.C. Durfee High School of Fall River, Mass., who have generously shared Mike's time with me during the writing of this book.

David Cleveland, Kevin Garganta, Richard and Debra Valcourt, and Dr. Melvin Yoken for their interest and encouragement.

My friend, Jim Rogers, a local businessman, who, as president of the Fall River chapter for fifteen years has helped over 2,000 students go on to higher education.

DEDICATION

This book is dedicated to the many people who believe in the concept that America is stronger and better served when citizens appreciate our priceless freedom and work toward the fulfillment of the dream of democracy.

To those of you whom I know, and the thousands of people whom I have never met, who work and continue to give hope and opportunity to our greatest assets–the future leaders of our communities and country–I give my heartfelt thanks and appreciation.

I hope my story will inspire you to become involved in a CSFA Dollars for Scholars chapter, if there is one in your community, or to start a chapter if there is not one.

CSFA is a unique national organization whose purpose is to help students by giving them hope, opportunity, and scholarships to go on to higher education.

Recently, I stopped by our local library and asked if they had any books that discussed what is good about America. They admitted that they didn't have any, and added that, in fact, nobody had ever asked for such a text before.

That's why I am writing this book. There is a lot of good in this country and there are many, many good people committed to the dream of democracy.

This book is dedicated to those Americans who are trying to leave this country a better place than we found it. I hope that it will inspire and motivate you to become involved and to feel there is something you also can do for your community.

As Rev. James G. Keller said: "Don't curse the darkness ... Light a candle!"

I believe CSFA can be that candle. At least it's my way of trying to leave our country a little better than I found it.

Irving A. Fradkin
Fall River, Massachusetts

"Some men see things as they are and say, 'Why?'I dream things that never were and say, 'Why not?'"

- *Robert Kennedy*

CHAPTER 1
THE DREAM TAKES HOLD

What a difference a few years make! I remember when cars were rare, when the streets were safe to walk at night, and when radio plays encouraged morality.

As a young child growing up in the Depression Era, my life was uneventful -- at least by today's standards. There were not many programs for children, so I spent most of my time after school playing ball out on the streets of Chelsea, Massachusetts.

Drugs were unheard of in Chelsea, violence and crime were rare, and I could walk down the street at any time of night without feeling threatened or afraid.

I also had the security of a good, traditional home, with a mother and father who cared for the seven of us children. My father worked as a baker for 12 to 14 hours a day to put food on the table and to provide an education for the children who wanted one.

Yet, with four sisters and two brothers, hand-me-downs were not unusual. As the baby of the family, sometimes my jackets were a little worn and my knickers were kind of big, but we kept warm when the New England weather turned cold.

We always had something on the table. Unlike today, there were no supermarkets, so we were limited to what we could get from the corner store. Whatever we had, whether a roasted chicken or just some soup, my mother made sure we never left the house hungry.

Looking back, I guess we were fortunate, not only to have food and clothing, but to have a family who cared.

By example, my father taught me the importance of caring for the family and working hard, but he also talked to me often of his dream and his love for America.

Abraham Fradkin, the baker, had a deep love for this country. He called this land a Golden Medina, using the Jewish word for a golden world. He left Russia because of the anti-semitism that existed then as it exists today. Russia was not the place to bring up a family and plan for his children's future. It took a great deal of courage to leave Russia to seek his future in America as he realized he would never again see his parents and siblings.

This is true of all refugees today -- Cambodians, Vietnamese, Armenians, Cubans, and others who have come to this country. They were persecuted because of economic conditions or religious beliefs. People the world over want some common things -- a better life for themselves and their families. America can give them this opportunity.

Our father would often remind the seven of us that we had freedom in America -- a freedom that wasn't possible in his native Russia. He often spoke of the rich soil of freedom which exists in the United States to nurture its people, in stark contrast in the dry turf of a dictatorship where freedom cannot grow.

As we grew up, we began to understand what our father meant when he told us that there really was no such thing as a self-made man. He explained to us that a person can't do anything by himself, but with work and determination, people can achieve just about anything in America.

Like most immigrants, my father came to this country from Russia with a desire to improve himself. To do so, he usually went to work at 12 o'clock at night and came home at two o'clock in the afternoon. You could see how tired he was by watching him slowly climb each step, and drop wearily into his chair. But no matter how tired or busy he was, he would take time to spend with his children.

By the time I was 10, I was working in my father's bakery shop on Saturdays. To be honest, it was more like play. I loved fooling around with frosting cupcakes and filling donuts. By the time I would leave, my face and apron displayed more frosting than the pastry did, and I had eaten more donuts than I had made.

I remember, too, the delight of making whipped cream and putting it on a hot cupcake or a turnover. It was a great time in my life. There's no question about it. I had plenty of love, lots of fun, and lots of friends.

As with most young people, I felt invincible. But then, at the age of 15, I played one game of sandlot football too many. I slipped and fell. When I did, the head of my right thigh bone slipped out of position.

In those days, doctors didn't know how to handle this type of injury. Today, all they do is put a nail in the bone, and secure it into position. In my day, they manipulated it, trying to move it back where it belonged. Afterwards, they put a cast on me from my waist down to the ankle. I wore the cast for four months, used crutches for the next six or eight months, and then was fit with a brace.

Even before I hurt my leg, I was quite a shy young man. Like many boys at that time, I played almost exclusively with males. In fact, I didn't say 'hello' to a girl until I was in the ninth grade.

After I hurt my hip, I withdrew into kind of a shell. Going to high school on crutches for three months, and then wearing a brace, definitely cramped my social life.

I've always thought, however, that getting hurt at that age helped make me more aware of the pain of others.

Even today, I always try to help someone who is on crutches or in a cast.

The accident also changed my career goals. I always figured I would follow in my father's footsteps, continuing his ownership of the bakery. After my injury, however, it quickly became clear that I would not be able to stand for the hours necessary to become a baker, so the next thing was to find something else that would motivate me.

As if my hip injury weren't enough of a challenge, my eyesight also was failing. At first, I didn't realize that I needed glasses. I thought my eyes were just tired and not focusing correctly, but when I got my glasses the whole world opened up to me.

I could see again. When my vision cleared, so did my future. I decided to become an optometrist and to help others to see as I had been helped.

Right out of high school, I went into the Massachusetts College of Optometry. My father made sure I had the funds to go through, even though tuition then was about $300 or $350 a year. At the time, that was about two months pay for him.

While in school, I worked nights and weekends to help my father. Sometimes I would be at the bakery for 20 hours straight. By the end of that time, the pain from my leg brace would make walking up the stairs a chore.

I enjoyed my optometric training. I had a good time in school. But even then, I was aware of my responsibility to others.

When I was a senior, I was elected treasurer of my college fraternity. During initiation night, I remember going by the room where the pledges were being initiated. To my surprise, I didn't hear any fun or laughter. When I looked in, what I saw shocked me. A group of second--

year students were paddling the hell out of the new pledges.

I yelled bloody murder because that's not fun. It hurts. I got really mad at them and insisted they stop the paddling. Later, at my urging, our society passed a law that prohibited paddling, and I was pleased that we were able to enforce that.

In college, I continued to have problems with my hip. I went to see a leading orthopedist who told me about a new method of grinding out the hip socket and putting a cup in. Although the doctor told me that the procedure would give me a great deal of relief from my discomfort, I found the operation and recovery were difficult.

After the operation, I had to spend eight weeks in bed, then a while longer on crutches. At first, I was disappointed, but the time I spent in my recovery gave me a chance to really get to know my mother for the first time.

When I was a kid, I had barely noticed her while I was busy playing ball or dating girls. But now, I was able to learn about all my mother had gone through on her way to America.

My father had come to this country from Russia in 1912. In 1917, he finally made enough money to send for my mother and the five children.

It wasn't as simple as getting on a plane and meeting my father in the new country. The six travelers had to cross Europe from Russia to get to Amsterdam, Holland. Once there, at the sea coast, they were able to board a ship.

During this trek across Germany, my mother was put in jail. She had stolen some wood because she needed fuel to make a fire to keep her children warm. My oldest sister, who was 12 at the time, went to the German in charge and was able to get my mother out.

The weary travelers finally made the last boat and got here in 1917, arriving in this country just before America got into the war. My brother, Bill, was born here in 1918, and I was born in 1921.

Getting to know my mother was a marvelous thing. As a child, I had seen her get up early every morning to make sure we all had food, and I knew I was sure fortunate to have a mother like her. But after learning about her journey to America, I also realized what guts it takes for people to leave their country because they want freedom so badly.

No matter what country a person's ancestors came from, those people came to America because they didn't have freedom where they were and they wanted better lives for themselves and their children.

Leaving the country that you were born in takes courage, and that's the type of people who made this country great. We, who benefitted from their courage, sometimes don't realize what it means that they came to this country so they could make a better life for us.

Learning what my mother had gone through gave me a clear and insightful understanding of what it means to be an American. Her stories made clear to me that government can deny freedom, wipe out assets, and take away lives. I felt lucky to be an American.

At about the same time, news of the Holocaust began to reach the United States in 1942, which was when I had my Smith-Petersen cup put in my hip. During my convalescence, I started to read about the horrors happening in Germany and elsewhere in the world. Before this, I had never bothered with history or even concerned myself with what was going on in other countries. I began to read not only newspaper accounts of World War II but also histories of other struggles.

My reading made me realize just how lucky we were to live in America. I began to understand all the marvelous things that could be done in the name of freedom if people were given a chance to exercise their right to do something good.

Especially at that time, America was the mecca for people to come to because, even with no education, and despite the struggle to learn a new language, they would be given an opportunity to exercise whatever God-given ability they had to try to make a better living for themselves.

So many marvelous people in this country came here with few possessions and little education. Yet, look at what they have done to build the magnificent country we have. To me, that is why America is the greatest country that was ever conceived, because here, we have the soil of liberty. The sad part is that the people who are now reaping the great benefit do not always realize how fortunate they are.

In 1943 I graduated from optometry school, studied for boards, and passed them. At the time, I felt that Boston was pretty well saturated with optometrists, but I wanted to stay close to home. I decided to find a community and open a practice somewhere within 30 miles of Boston.

I visited a few cities, which was not easy because I still was on crutches. One day I contacted Joseph Clark, an optician in Fall River, Massachusetts, who heard I was looking for a position.

He offered to help me get started in Fall River, but I felt I had to be honest and tell him that I was still using crutches to get around. For some people in those days, the inability to walk without help would have been looked on as a problem. Joe Clark didn't feel that way.

"That's okay," he said, "you can examine even if you're on crutches."

I opened my practice with $700 loaned to me by my father. Sure, I had to buy used equipment, eat crackers and a glass of milk for lunch, and scrimp to make it, but it was worth it. I had a profession and I felt like I was part of the community.

Right from my first visit, I loved Fall River. Here was a community that had trees and grass, which I had seen little of in congested Chelsea. But more than the scenery, I met a nice group of people.

"This is the type of community I'd like to live in," I thought as I walked through North Park and watched the sun paint the sky glorious colors over the Taunton River.

So I settled in Fall River. While I was trying to make a living, I also got involved with youth. The young people were so magnificent. They were idealistic and beautiful to work with.

While most of the men my age were serving in World War II, I was declared 4-F because of my hip injury. There was a need for men in many local leadership positions, and I got involved with the New England Council of Young Judeans, as well as four or five other youth groups during war time.

Although I couldn't serve in the military, I was able to use my time and my talent to encourage young people to make a better life for themselves. At the same time, I became more interested and involved in Judaism, attending national and district conventions.

One day in June of 1946, I was an usher at a friend's wedding in Boston. As I was leaving Chelsea on the street car to return to Fall River the next day, I scanned the passengers, as I always would, to see if I knew anyone.

Suddenly, my head snapped back when I saw this blue-eyed blonde. I had known Charlotte Sheinfield from my youth in Chelsea, but I had never dated her. In fact, I had hardly dated any girls from Chelsea.

But I said to my sister, who was standing at my side on the street car, "That's for me."

To this day, I still call it my street car named "desire."

When we got out of the street car at the last stop in Maverick Station, I stepped up behind this young lady, and we started a conversation.

We dated and seven dates later, on August 25, we were engaged. We were married on November 27.

It was kind of fast, but I had an absolutely marvelous year with Charlotte. After more than 45 years, I can honestly say that I am one of the very lucky people who would marry the same person again. She's everything I desired and everything I wanted. We still have a wonderful marriage, three great children and three marvelous grandchildren.

After we married, I struggled to make a living in Fall River. We had an apartment where I also had my office. For a while, I also opened another office in the Flint section of Fall River. I would take my portable equipment back and forth between the two offices for examinations.

I really wasn't making much money, but I ran back and forth as best I could to try to make a living. After we had our first child, I went into the real estate business in addition to my optometric practice to try to make a better living. At the time, you could buy houses for $12,000 to $15,000, with only a thousand dollars down. In time, I pyramided the houses so that eventually I owned 18 houses.

As Fall River became our home, I became involved in community activities. As a member of the Junior Chamber of Commerce, for example, I became part of the Clean-Up Committee and remember pushing a broom around the old City Hall, which was located where Route 195 now cuts a path through the center of the city. What we did wasn't glamorous, but we made the city just a little better for all of its residents.

Later, I was appointed to the Traffic Commission and served as its chairman. For the first time, I was in an official position, and I think I did a few good things.

The first thing was to turn over my $25 monthly stipend to an officer whose purpose was to give us direction and assistance. I didn't want to take pay for community service.

I also led the way with other community improvements. At the time, the crosswalks were painted by hand, and I found out that a machine had been produced which could do the job much easier, dried instantly and made the job less injurious to the workers. I also instituted the idea that any new apartments had to have at least one parking space. People actually used to fight over parking spaces.

Eventually, at the urging of some friends, I ran for the school committee. It would be a fateful decision.

"If a nation expects to be ignorant and free, in a state of civilization, it expects what never was and never will be."

- *Thomas Jefferson*

CHAPTER 2
DOLLARS FOR SCHOLARS BEGINS

I was feeling about as gray as the granite mill buildings which once housed the great textile industry long since gone South. At age 38, I had lost my bid for school committee. As I walked through Fall River's downtown in 1957, I thought perhaps the people who left had the right idea.

After all, I had worked hard meeting people in this city of neighborhoods. I had gone to the Portuguese clubs on Columbia Street and to the French socials in the Flint; from the South End to Steep Brook, I had visited and talked about my ideas on education.

Many people agreed with my suggestion that schools be opened for use by the community, and that cities and towns share building plans to save on design costs. And just about everybody thought the best idea I proposed was that a scholarship program should be established to help provide a college education for anyone who wanted one.

Running for office seemed like a good idea, but now, I wasn't sure. Despite the support for my ideas, I didn't get the votes I needed. I had just about arrived at my office when I spotted John Cabral, the son of my receptionist Isabelle, running toward me.

"Dr. Fradkin," he called, "I just wanted to tell you how sorry I am you lost the election. I was counting on you and your scholarship program to help me get through college."

We talked for a while, and I thought about what he had said. I may have lost the election, I immediately concluded, but I did not lose the cause. I decided that I didn't have to be an elected official to keep my promise. As a private citizen, I would work to start a community scholarship program.

Yet, when I'd bring up the subject to others, they would either ask "What's in it for you?" or "Why bother."

Those comments made me think back to my young patients. Whenever I would ask them about education, many would say that they were going to quit school because there was no future. They could not afford to go on to college, so they would not bother to finish high school.

"What a shame," I thought, "It's not the oil in the ground which is America's greatest asset. It is the minds of our young people that should not be wasted."

Had I been wealthy, I would have set up a trust fund. Then I thought about the idea of democracy. What if many people donated just a little. That could work.

If everyone in Fall River would just give a dollar -- one dollar -- then there would be enough money to provide an education to everyone who wanted one.

I had the dream -- and my father's belief that every person has an obligation to give something back to this country for the opportunities that have been given to them. I was determined to begin repaying my debt to democracy.

By December, the hurt left by the election loss had been replaced by the excitement of establishing a scholarship program. I invited ten people to a meeting at the Hotel Mellen across from the library in downtown Fall River. Only four showed up.

Still, I was happy to meet with Ed Delaney and Fred Dube of the *Fall River Herald News*, as well as civic leaders, Maury Kusinitz and Ruth Merritt. They gave me encouragement and promised to call on some of their friends.

In January, there was another meeting of friends and neighbors at the International Ladies Garment Workers' Union near the Post Office. Several more people showed up and it seemed my dream might come true after all. A Citizens' Scholarship Foundation was taking shape.

While recovering from surgery for a deviated septum, I had plenty of time to get on the phone and make call after call after call. Many paid off.

I sent letters to every politician and dignitary I thought would be interested. Soon I was even getting replies and support.

One day, when the mail came, I flipped through the envelopes. Maybe someone would send us a dollar and become a member of Citizens' Scholarship Foundation.

After tossing the first few utility bills onto the table, I came upon a return address that made my face drop. The letter was from Eleanor Roosevelt.

"I was interested to get your letter and to learn of the effort being made in your community to make your people more aware of the opportunities and advantages of a college education. I congratulate you and am happy to send you a dollar toward the effort," she wrote.

In the envelope was a crisp one dollar bill. The popular former First Lady became the first person to subscribe to the Citizens' Scholarship Foundation.

Soon other endorsements -- and dollars -- came in. Religious leaders supported the program, including Rabbi Samuel Ruderman and Rev. Finley Keech. Bishop James

L. Connolly's endorsement was carried in the *Fall River Herald News*:

"Here enclosed find my contribution, small enough, for the establishment of a Scholarship Fund in Greater Fall River," wrote the Bishop. "Since your demands are so modest, I feel quite confident that the community as a whole will respond generously and trust that many of our deserving young men and women will benefit by the scholarships through the medium of this fund."

I went on the radio to ask for the community's support. I read a list of endorsements which included not only Mrs. Roosevelt, but also President Dwight D. Eisenhower, Senator John F. Kennedy, Senator Everett Saltonstall, Dr. James R. Killian, Representative Joseph W. Martin, Jr., Governor Foster Furcolo, and Secretary of Health, Education and Welfare Marion B. Folsom.

I also told the listening audience that a representative of *Time* and *Life* magazines would be taking pictures and that WJAR television from Providence, Rhode Island was planning a story in March.

"Friends, this is your golden opportunity to help your children towards a higher education in the college or school of their choice, for a membership fee of only a dollar a year," I said.

President Eisenhower not only endorsed the program, but said he would send a telegram the night of the kickoff membership meeting. He was true to his word.

About 75 people attended the first official meeting of Citizens' Scholarship Foundation of Greater Fall River at the International Ladies' Garment Workers' Union building on February 20, 1958 and one of the first things they heard was a message from the President of the United States.

"It is good to learn of the scholarship project begun by the citizens' of Greater Fall River. This is a splendid example of the kind of increased local concern for education needed in communities throughout the nation.

"In order to achieve the fruitful goals of democracy, everyone must help our talented young people develop their abilities to the utmost," he wrote.

Eisenhower's scientific adviser, Dr. James R. Killian, former president of the Massachusetts Institute of Technology, also enrolled as a member of CSF.

"If we are to maintain leadership in this century of science, we must be sure that we devote an adequate amount of our energy and resources to the cultivation of talent and intellectual accomplishment," Killian noted. "It is felt that the program envisioned by your committee is taking a forward step in the accomplishment of the necessary objectives."

In endorsing the drive, Senator Kennedy cited "the imperative need for broadening our financial base and enriching the curricular content of our educational system," adding, "I wish this splendid community effort every success."

Congressman Martin also joined the effort.

"I know of no community effort of greater importance than the stimulation of advanced learning among our youth," he said. "It deserves the support of our citizens because the need is great and urgent."

Superintendent of Schools William Lynch spoke about the need for scholarship assistance in the community, and stressed that many would be helped by the program.

The organizers also set a five-fold purpose before the membership.

The first was to send 15 or more young people to college ... *or its equivalent*. I always felt that this option was important because it allowed the Foundation to fund trade and nursing school students.

I believed all young people wanting to better themselves should be included. Those who wish to go on to scientific professional schools, who work with their hands, or who serve with their heart should get the same support as those who wish to attend a four-year college.

The group's second goal was to make the college preparatory course at B.M.C. Durfee High School, the city's public high school, more accessible since more scholarships would be available.

Third, CSF wanted to offer new hope to citizens who would be watching the grades of their children more closely because the means of higher education would be available to them.

A fourth goal was to make parents aware of the increasing lack of scholarship monies available from colleges.

The fifth was to eventually establish a branch of the Massachusetts State University in the Greater Fall River area.

Elections were held and I became the first president of Citizens' Scholarship Foundation. Ruth Merritt was vice president; Martha Isherwood, secretary; Daniel J. McCarthy, corresponding secretary; Thomas Ellison, treasurer; and Leo J. F. Donovan; auditor.

Superintendent of Schools Lynch was named chairman of the Board of Directors, to be comprised of presidents of all "civic-minded organizations".

Committees and their chairs were also announced. They included: Membership, Paul Gonsalves; Bylaws, Probate Judge Beatrice Hancock Mullaney and Attorney Abraham Tulchin; Scholarship Awards, Lloyd H. Dixon, Ambrose F. Keeley, Edward J. Kaylor; Publicity, Richard Larter; Speaker's Bureau, Attorney Roland G. Desmarais; Program, Dr. Raymond Connors; Finance, Roger L. Currant, George W. Graham, Leeds Burchard, and John S. Brayton, Jr.

As I shook hands and said goodbye, I thought about all the support from the national leaders. Then I looked at the roster of the officers and committees just approved by the membership. The names read like a Who's Who of Fall River. There were lawyers and teachers, doctors and judges, elected officials and business owners.

My dream of a community supported scholarship program was coming true, and I was happy to be elected the first president, but on my way home, I remember wondering if the people of this city would each be willing to part with just one dollar to help a young person. I sure hoped they would.

"Education best fulfills its high purpose when responsibility for education is kept close to the people it serves, when it is rooted in the home, nurtured in the community and sustained by a rich variety of public, private and individual resources."

- President Dwight D. Eisenhower

CHAPTER 3
THE COMMUNITY RESPONDS

Every day the mail seemed to bring better news. Sure there were bills, but also in the box were letters from the Kiwanis Club, from the International Ladies Garment Workers' Union, and from the Amvets. As important, there were notes and dollars from members of the community, people I didn't even know or would ever meet. All had the same concern: that the youth of 1958 would not have to work as hard or as long as their parents.

Despite the recession which saw Fall River's population slide from 120,000 to 103,000, with an average annual wage of a little more than $3,000, people came through.

I knew they would. I knew that people would understand that our priceless heritage of freedom and democracy can best be preserved through an educated citizenry.

Just one week after the official campaign began, Citizens' Scholarship Foundation had raised $1,000, mostly through $1 memberships. It was well on its way to reaching its goal of 15 scholarships of $100 to $300 a year.

But it's not just the money, I would tell people again and again. What's unique about Citizens' Scholarship Foundation is the fact that people care enough to ensure an education for the young people in their community. That's what's important. This is a hand up, not a hand out!

The message of democracy was heard in City Hall Chambers. Scholarship Week was proclaimed by Mayor John M. Arruda and City Council President Andrew J. Farrissey.

"The Citizens' Scholarship Foundation of Greater Fall River, in its effort to raise, by public subscription, monies to help provide college scholarships to deserving high school graduates who are without means to otherwise attain their goal, deserves the support of all of our citizens," Arruda noted.

He called on the public to support the drive to help in "the re-birth of the great City of Fall River" through higher education for its children.

Farrissey agreed.

"I believe that such a fund will prove beneficial in many ways and will be one step forward toward a brighter and more prosperous city," he said.

Local business leaders agreed. From the independent neighborhood stores which made up the Fall River Grocers Association to the Loomfixers Union, to the many city workers, support came pouring in.

One day, a call came in from Thomas A. Rodgers, Jr. president of Globe Manufacturing. He, too, pursued a dream, but his was to found a local company, a company that eventually became one of the nation's largest manufacturers of rubber thread.

Rodgers told me that his company had a donation to present to Citizens' Scholarship Foundation. Rodgers and Walter Ramanowicz, Globe production manager, presented John C. Sullivan, our Foundation publicity director, and me a check representing 100 percent support by the workers in all three shifts. As if that wasn't enough, Rodgers said that the company matched the donation.

"There is a need for advanced education of high school pupils here," Rodgers suggested, adding that it is often necessary for Globe to search elsewhere to find the highly-skilled scientists needed for the complex manufacturing systems of the 1950's.

Back in my office, I went to pull out another membership card from my drawer for another patient who came in for eyeglasses and left sharing my vision for a better educated population.

The philosophy seemed to work. Some people stopped by my office and said they couldn't afford a dollar but would bring in 25 cents a week until they completed their membership payment.

"Let the big scholarship programs get their support from corporations, alumni and tax revenues, Fall River's people can take care of their own," I said to the volunteers as they began to work the telephones, canvassing people.

"People who have contributed feel that they have a stake in higher education," I said, "And students who used to give up hope when they got to be juniors in high school are now more likely to stick with it."

My enthusiasm was spreading!

"Hey Doc," a man yelled from his truck, "Here's a buck - and thanks. It's great to be able put a kid through school."

He jumped back in his truck and rumbled down the road.

Another day as I headed for work, a man stopped me. From the pocket of his soiled pants, the worker pulled a crumbled one dollar bill.

"You know, I quit school to work the mills. Never had a chance to go to college. I hope this helps some kid so he will never have to work as hard as me," he said, and continued walking down the street.

Donations poured in from the Catholic and Protestant church groups, from the Jewish temple and service clubs. Workers at Chinese restaurants and all night diners sent in donations. Housewives rang doorbells and sold memberships at Women's Guild meetings and Hadassah socials.

Because the scholarships were planned, not just for Fall River students, but also for young people in the surrounding communities of Somerset, Swansea, Westport, Assonet and Tiverton, Rhode Island, support came in from those quarters as well.

The Spectator, a weekly newspaper serving Somerset and Swansea, two towns across the Taunton River from the city, joined the local paper, The *Fall River Herald News*, in endorsing the project.

"It would be difficult to think of a more appealing project than the Citizens' Scholarship Fund of Greater Fall River. Or of a more appealing feature than the fact that anybody can do his full duty towards it for a single dollar," a *Spectator* editorial said.

Edward C. Suspiro was named first chairman of the Somerset scholarship drive, and he mobilized a group led by precinct chairmen Raymond McConnell, Stephen J. Biello, Theodore J. Danis, Dr. Alvin Servita, George Raposa, Raymond McGee, Frank Duffy, and Eugene Rutkowski.

With the approval of the Selectmen, Sunday, April 13, 1958 was declared SOS Day, meaning "Support Our Scholarships" or "Save Our Students." The door-to-door campaign not only raised funds for the program, but Somerset, in effect, also became the first community beyond the borders of Fall River to conduct a door-to-door solicitation.

"This is an opportunity for the people to solve their own problems on their own without outside interference,"

Attorney James W. Killoran, town moderator, said to a gathering of the Somerset committee, "It has been a tradition of Americans to help themselves whenever the need arises."

In the spring of 1958, as funds continued to mount, so did optimism that even more students would be helped than was originally planned.

With the excitement came more endorsements.

"As time passes and higher education becomes more of a necessity than a luxury, scholarships are bound to become more numerous," a *Fall River Herald News* editorial pointed out. "At present the city as a whole is in the debt of the private groups that are helping to make college a reality for so many of our deserving students."

From New York came the congratulations of Malcolm P. Aldrich, a well-known former athlete from the city's B.M.C. Durfee High School and now a successful businessman. He read of his home town's scholarship program in the *New York Times*.

"This is the self-reliant, typically New England way of solving such problems. I hope that the idea will be taken up enthusiastically by industry and individuals in Fall River and in many other localities throughout the country," he wrote. "In order to have a small part in the inauguration of this fine work, I am enclosing my check for $100."

As the sun set over the Taunton River on the evening of our next CSF meeting, I made my way home. "Tonight we'll know," I thought to myself. "Tonight we'll see just how many young people we can help."

At the meeting, we added up the last pile of contributions. Some were checks, some were coins, but all came from the heart, I thought. When we were through, the whole group sat back and smiled. The $4500 raised in the last six months was enough to give 24 scholarships to students from area high schools.

Then I took off my glasses and rubbed my eyes.

"Now, comes the hard part," I said, "how do we decide who gets the help?"

"Each time a man stands up for an ideal or acts to improve the lot of others or strikes out against injustice, he sends forth a tiny ripple of hope, and crossing each other, these ripples build a current that can sweep down the mightiest walls of oppression and resistance."

- *Robert F. Kennedy*

CHAPTER 4
THE PROGRAM WORKS

"In deciding who will get the scholarships, we have to come up with a way to eliminate favoritism and partiality," I advised the Citizens' Scholarship Foundation officers that night at our meeting.

After considering several ideas, we decided to number each application so that no one except the chairman would know the identity of the student until the judging was final. We also decided that the students must live in the Massachusetts' communities of Fall River, Assonet, Swansea, Somerset, Westport or in adjacent Tiverton, Rhode Island, or have graduated from a high school in one of the localities.

Students had to provide a list of colleges, universities or other schools that they would like to attend, but it was not limited to four-year schools. Applicants to technical institutions and teacher training colleges, nursing schools or junior colleges were also invited to apply.

"Since God has given each of us a range of talents, let us try to help provide a method to develop these talents," I said.

Once the candidates were accepted by the schools, they had to notify the committee of their definite choices as well as provide a list of other scholarships received.

"We don't want one person to get all the help while another goes without," I said. "If we know applicants do not need the assistance because they've found scholarships elsewhere, that frees up funds to help someone else."

Another board member suggested that the applicants should rank in the top half of their classes, and another stressed that need must be a consideration. These were also agreed upon.

A point system was devised, and while record and character were considered, need was weighed the heaviest. Applicants were given 45 points for greatest need, 35 for being an All-A student, 10 points for such unusual family circumstances as sickness or death, 5 points for leadership potential and 5 points for efforts made to provide self-help through part-time work.

A deadline of April 29 was set, and Lloyd Dixon, a pillar of the community, insurance executive, was nominated to oversee the committee of seven judges. No one could think of a better man.

Applications arrived almost daily and the group labored to review them. In the end, the names represented most of Fall River's diverse ethnic population as well as all creeds and economic levels.

The first awards were made on June 9, 1958 in the Technical High School Auditorium at B.M.C. Durfee High School. College banners with the names of every school that the recipients would attend were hung on the curtains behind the speakers. The mood was festive and the auditorium was packed.

I was so excited just looking at the curtains behind the stage. The banners were from impressive schools like Yale, but also from nearby nursing and trade schools. The wide variety of colors and pennants were reflected in the diverse group of citizens that made up the audience. We had reached across the lines that often divide a city and brought people of all ethnic and social groups together.

"This was strictly a community effort, and it shows when we, as a united people, work for a good cause, no job is too great," I told the audience of students and parents, educators and friends.

Dean Judson T. Shaplin of the Harvard Graduate School of Education was the main speaker. He was joined on stage by Dixon, Dr. Alan G. Simpson, Edward J. Kaylor, Francis W. Buswell, Fall River School Superintendent William S. Lynch, and all executive committee members of the foundation. The PTA orchestra performed under the direction of Joseph S. Raposo.

In his remarks, Shaplin credited federal and state government as well as industry for their efforts in providing aid but emphasized that it is the local community that can most fairly decide which students need help.

"You in Fall River have brought a broader citizen interest in a great problem. And I have not known a group offering a higher inspiration for higher education," he said.

Shaplin also pointed out that there was a great need in light of increasing costs. He recalled that tuition at Harvard cost him, as an undergraduate, $400 a year, which, with living expenses, brought the total cost for the academic year up to $1,100. In 1958, he said, that cost has escalated to $1,250 for tuition alone, and, with living costs, to $2,500 a year.

The result, he suggested, was that education will eventually reach a point where only the wealthy would be able to send their children to college and pay their way. In order to keep education as an opportunity for all people, he advised that other communities follow the new concept developed in Fall River. Little could I have imagined as he spoke that some day hundreds of other American communities would also be forming their own Citizens'

Scholarship Foundations, known as Dollars for Scholars chapters.

"This is a first step," Shaplin said, "and it is a magnificent thing in and of itself." How prophetic he was!

Finally, it was time to announce the awards. Each young person was called up to the stage to receive his or her scholarship award, which ranged from $50 to $300.

Receiving awards were Florence M. Bell, Geraldine M. Cahill, R. Judson Carlberg, Joan M. Collard, Lucy S. Dubiel, Mary E. Dunn, Catherine V. Gesner, Catherine M. Goulet, John R. Harty, Argirios A. Kuliopolis, Carolyn A. Lenaghan, Ruth M. Lincoln, Geraldine M. Mendes, Joseph Morais, Georgette A. Pereira, Vernon L. Phillips, Jr., Rose Marie Ponte, Roger D. Raymond, William K. Reilly, Dale R. M. Silva, Walter R. Silvia, Clare E. Sinotte, and Jeffrey S. Trust.

These young people not only graduated from a cross-section of private and public schools in several cities and towns, but had also been accepted by a wide variety of schools ranging from local colleges to internationally known universities. From Bridgewater State Teachers College, Saint Anne's Hospital School of Nursing and Bradford Durfee College of Technology to Brown University, the University of Notre Dame, and Otterbein College in Ohio, the list was impressive.

I remember sitting on the stage and thinking: this is more than a scholarship program; it is an example of democracy at work.

Every name on the list seemed to have a story behind it -- a story about good people trying to improve their situation. An article in the *Ladies Home Journal* recorded some of the stories.

"Education is a wonderful thing. I never had much of it," a gray-haired Portuguese man told the writer from the magazine while they sat in the five room, $20 a month, cold-water apartment, which the man and his wife shared with their two children.

"I went right to work in a cotton mill. I'm glad my children can get an education. I know how good it is to know things about the world all around. My daughter will make a good teacher. She likes little kids," he continued. "I hope when my son gets older, the people of Fall River will think he is good and will help him get a scholarship too. He thinks he would like to be a dentist."

Across the state line in Tiverton, Rhode Island, a young girl feeding chickens outside a farmhouse also told her story to the magazine. As long as she can remember, she said, she wanted to be a nurse.

"I want to help people. But I thought right after high school, I would have to go to work. I never dreamed I could ever really be a nurse," she said. "I won a Fall River Citizens' Scholarship and now I am studying to be a nurse. Sometimes I rub my eyes when I am in the hospital and wonder if it can be true and yet it is true."

The message was not lost on the young people, who became ambassadors for the program. One of them, William K. Reilly, who went on to serve as Director of the Environmental Protection Agency, published his view in the opinion column of the local newspaper, the *Fall River Herald News*.

"American education remains, despite perennial lobbying for increased national intervention and help, a local responsibility. Thus, only a movement at the grass-roots level is capable of rising to the crisis which Russian progress has precipitated," he wrote in part.

"It is a credit to the people of Fall River that they indeed have the potential of just such a movement in the Citizens' Scholarship Foundation. As one of the 24 recipients, I am especially appreciative of the efforts of Fall Riverites to increase the scope and broaden the financial base of its awards," Reilly continued.

Not long after the college banners were taken down from the auditorium curtain, and the thank you notes put away, work began on the next campaign.

Once again, $1 memberships in Citizens' Scholarship Foundation were sold; but this year, the board had some other ideas. For a minimum contribution of $100, organizations could become Scholarship Sponsors and awards would be presented in their group's name.

"We hope to expand the number of individual memberships up to 10,000 and enlist every club and business firm in town to sponsor scholarships in their own names," I wrote in a letter to the civic groups and businesses.

I visited just about every place of worship in the city and asked each one to donate $100 to establish a scholarship in the name of their parish or congregation. At first, some clergy agreed, but only if the award would be given to a person of their faith.

I refused to guarantee that outcome as it was impossible to do so because of the selection process. I explained that all applications would be numbered so that decisions would be completely free of partiality.

When they understood that their young people would be neither favored nor discriminated against, most of them opened their checkbooks and offered a donation.

I remember thinking how this could be a way to break down ethnic barriers. People really want to help others if all are really treated equally.

During my lunch hour, I would pick up the phone and schedule visits to the countless sewing shops and manufacturing firms that occupied the towering mills where textile equipment once roared.

"Can you give a dollar to help a young person?" I would ask the workers, more often than not through a translator.

When the employees' collection was completed, the $57 or $80 would be turned over to the Citizens' Scholarship Foundation, and most of the time the owner would contribute the difference to establish a $100 scholarship in the company's name.

It always amazed and impressed me that people who never had the chance to go to school really understand the need for an education.

On the night of the awards presentation, each company and organization would send a representative to award the scholarship. There were police and fire departments, Chinese restaurants and civic clubs, sewing shops and social groups all different, yet all the same in their willingness to help young people. It was truly America in action!

As part of the scholarship process, each recipient would be asked to write a thank you note to the company or organization that awarded the grant. Most of the donors became so aware of just how important the scholarship was that they continued to renew the donation.

By September 10, 1958, pledges and donations had already surpassed the $4,500 raised during the first campaign. And there was more good news; a Youth Branch was established. Like the program itself, it began innocently enough.

When a B.M.C. Durfee High School student, Adrianne Levine, asked me how she could help, I suggested talking to other teens and parents and maybe raising some money.

On the way home, she ran into a friend who said, "Let's have a radio marathon."

The telephone company ran some phone lines, and radio personalities urged people to give. As each pledge was made, a play money dollar was stapled to a huge sheet of cardboard which covered the street in front of City Hall.

"It was almost all paved by the time the day was over," she recalled. "We collected $1,400 altogether...that included what we got from the dance we held afterward, and, boy, it was quite a day."

Representatives from all eight high schools in greater Fall River joined together to form a board of directors for the Youth Branch. But in addition to raising funds for other young people, I stressed that their work would strengthen the organization and help combat juvenile delinquency.

"Give the youngsters a purpose, and they'll give it their all," I said, and I was not proven wrong. The projects they came up with were filled with the enthusiasm of youth."

James Friar and Jo-Ann Sampson co-chaired a "Beatnik Blast" at the Masonic Temple in Fall River, and both the decoration and dress were in keeping with a Greenwich Village coffee house.

In 1959 students in caps and gowns set up toll booths in the city to collect donations for Citizens' Scholarship Foundation. For about four hours a day, they manned the streets of Fall River. On their best day, they collected over $4,000 in four hours.

In November, the traditional Thanksgiving football rivalry had a new twist. The Durfee girls played the New Bedford, Massachusetts girls in a "Powder Puff" football game which benefitted CSF.

While local efforts continued, so did interest from other communities. People wanted to know about the program that had become known as the "Fall River Plan."

Newspapers and magazines from *Newsweek* to *Better Homes and Gardens* carried stories about the first national grass roots scholarship program and the young optometrist from Fall River with a dream. *Opticians of London*, a British publication, also reported the story.

Inquiries arrived from all 50 states, but the first community beyond Fall River to adopt Citizens' Scholarship Foundation as its own was Pittsfield, Massachusetts. Its prime mover was my own brother, Dr. William S. Fradkin.

"If you can do it in Fall River, we can do it here in Pittsfield," Bill told me.

And like I had done a year or so before, my brother went to the service clubs and to the schools of his community explaining the concept. When the Pittsfield chapter of the Citizens' Scholarship Foundation began, my brother Bill was elected president. Under his leadership, more young people were helped each year.

Seeing that the program could work in another community, I took the success in Pittsfield and used it as an example of how the Fall River Plan could be applied elsewhere.

After reading in the daily newspaper that the nearby Rhode Island towns of Barrington, Warren and Bristol were running out of scholarship money, I went to each community to speak about the Citizens' Scholarship Foundation. In May of 1959, Barrington created a chapter of CSF. Judge Fred B. Perkins headed the new group.

More than 1,000 inquiries arrived from all parts of the country. As interest in the program grew nationally, so did the number of applicants locally. By the application deadline, 97 Fall River area students had applied for assistance, almost 50 percent more than in the first year.

The good news was that 23 of the first year's scholarships in Fall River would be renewed, and another 25 graduating high school seniors would receive help. The additional awards were made possible by the $8,050 raised in 1959.

Again, the awards ceremony was a time for celebration and inspiration. Dr. J. Paul Mather, president of the University of Massachusetts, gave the address.

He stressed the importance of developing freedom of ability and personality as an individual, but warned that "such freedom comes from hard, monotonous work to develop the tools of the chosen trade for complete mastery of oneself."

Superintendent of Schools William Lynch again served as master of ceremonies. He noted that the idea of Citizens' Scholarship Foundation had touched the heart of democracy.

"It allows every citizen to participate in providing the generation to come with the tools for a better America through higher education," he suggested.

While I was elated that the number of scholarships had doubled, I told the group that my hope was that they could present another 25 in 1960. Then I urged them to aim for a total of 100 scholarships by 1961 to cover all four years of a college education.

As a way to recognize the many volunteers who had helped the program grow, we began to recognize individuals with a "John Q. Public" or "Jane Doe" scholarship. The honorees would come up from the audience and would wear a small bronze plaque citing the distinction as they handed out the scholarships. It was a nice way to recognize people who had helped our youth.

"Amazing," I thought as I walked out of the Durfee Technical Building doors onto June Street after the awards ceremony was over. "It's amazing how we've grown in such a short time."

More important than the numbers, however, was the fact that there was a sense of pride stirring in the city.

One day a call came in from Mayor John M. Arruda's office. New signs were going up at the entrances to the city. They read, "Welcome to Fall River -- The Scholarship City."

But the pride wasn't limited to Fall River. In Pittsfield, Gladys Wertman was busy waiting on tables at the Yellow Aster when she thought about the girl from across the street. Just the other day, the girl had asked for a donation for something called the Citizens' Scholarship Foundation of Pittsfield, and Wertman had given her $2.

After work, Wertman asked her son Ralph if he thought it was a good cause. He said he thought it was.

"If I give $100, will it be all right?" she asked.

"Mother, that would be wonderful," he said.

The next day, they presented the donation to CSF. The local paper ran the story under the headline: "Big Tip From a Waitress -- $102 for Scholarship Fund."

Not everyone was a believer. Although John M. Allen of the *Reader's Digest* would accept my collect calls and agreed that the program was of national interest, Robert O'Brien, the young reporter he sent to Fall River to write the story was very skeptical.

"I don't know why Mr. Allen sent me down here," he said, "but he told me to come down and interview you so here I am."

He went on to explain that his home town in Connecticut had an average income of $13,000 and he saw no value in scholarships of between $100 and $300.

Soon he learned that Fall River's average income was about $3,000 and that every recipient he interviewed was not only worthy but needy. He changed his mind.

"These people live from hand to mouth," he said. "Without your help they would not be able to go on to higher education. You are doing a great service, and I'm going to do a great story for you."

"He was true to his word," I thought as I flipped through the March 1962 *Reader's Digest* in my office. "I'll bet many people will appreciate the need and start chapters based on this article."

As more people heard of the Citizens' Scholarship Foundation programs, new doors opened. I would call the White House collect, and was even invited to meet President Eisenhower. Although the President was called away to a special meeting of the Senate, a special assistant offered me a tour of the White House.

"Imagine, me, the son of Russian immigrants visiting the President's home," I thought as we walked down a spacious hallway.

Suddenly, a handsome young man opened the door for me. It was the President's son, John Eisenhower. After some pleasantries, he smiled and went on his way.

As I left the grounds and walked down Pennsylvania Avenue, I thought that this really is an amazing country when the President's son and a baker's boy can shake hands and meet in a house owned by all the people.

Back in Fall River, I turned over the presidency of the group to Raymond L. Wilson. After two years of zealous work on the cause, it was time to turn my attention more to my practice and my family.

But still, I would close my office every Wednesday to give me a chance to speak about the Citizens' Scholarship Foundation. Even though I was a one man operation and could not produce any income on the days the office was closed, money has never been my God. What inspired me then and drives me now is the dream of democracy and the potential of CSFA. That vision is what also prompted me to accept no salary and to pay my own way as I went throughout the area speaking about the program and sharing the dream.

I would often explain to people that the idea behind this non-profit, non-salaried scholarship program is to provide the soil and the climate in which the ideals of democracy and brotherhood can take root and flourish.

The program not only provides scholarships for deserving students in need of financial assistance, I would remind them, but also provides lessons for the entire community in generosity, respect for education, and in civic pride.

It worked. In 1960, Fall River boosted its contributions to $18,000 with 67 students getting assistance.

But the number of students being helped in other areas was also inspiring. By 1960, the chapters in Fall River, Pittsfield, and Barrington were joined by those in the Massachusetts communities of Dighton-Rehoboth, Berkley-Freetown, Taunton and Wakefield, as well as the Rhode Island communities of Bristol, North Kingston, Warren and Warwick.

By the end of 1960, the message was clear. It was time to establish a Citizens' Scholarship Foundation of America, and the 11 founding chapters decided to meet.

"If you will it, it's no dream," I would say, recalling the words of Theodore Herzl, the founder of modern Zionism.

Still, what nerve I had to think that I, an ordinary, unknown person with no money or expertise in fund raising could start a national organization. Yet, I had a deep faith and trust in the people of America, and a willingness to try.

"We have the basis here of what will truly be the first national grass-roots scholarship program," I told the representatives of the founding chapters at our meeting. "I've got a tiger by the tail! There's no telling where this will end."

Dr. Fradkin leads the first organizational meeting of the potential formation of CSF of Greater Fall River. His wife Charlotte at his right is very much involved as well (1958).

First Scholarship Awards Night in Fall River, 24 recipients (1958).

Five of the first 24 scholarship awards recipients (1958).

Discussing formation of the second Citizens' Scholarship Foundation in Pittsfield, MA, with brother Bill Fradkin, and citizen volunteer (1959).

Soliciting support for scholarships from the optometrist's office (1959).

Successful dance fund-raiser for CSF of Fall River, organized by the youth branch. One thousand people attended (1959).

Awards committee for CSF of Fall River processing scholarship applications (1960).

Scholarship awards night for CSF of Fall River, 87 awards, third year of the program (1960).

Dr. Fradkin and his brother Bill discuss Citizens' Scholarship Foundation with Mass. House Majority Leader Joe Martin (1960).

The toll booth, a great fund-raising project for CSF. Raised $4,000 in four hours (1961). Marlene Fradkin with James Waring (above); Cheerleaders of Durfee High.

Scholarship awards night, 1961. Banners indicated colleges to be attended by many of the recipients.

$1,440 for scholarships in $10, $20, and $50 bills - sent anonymously - the FBI and the Police Department concluded that it was clean and honest money - the UP and AP sent the story nationally over the news wires, saying that Santa Claus came early that year! (December 1962)

Fall River Dollars for Scholars volunteers and Dr. Fradkin counting bills from the anonymous gift (December, 1962).

Dr. Fradkin receives key to the city of Fall River from Mayor Roland Desmarais, with Francis Buswell, President of CSF of Fall River looking on (1964).

"It's about time that we stopped teaching the kids that we owe them something. Teach them that they owe something to America, to other human beings and to God."

- Sam Levenson

CHAPTER 5
THE MOVE TO NATIONAL PROMINENCE

One Sunday night as I relaxed on my sofa, I watched Ed Sullivan introduce Sam Levenson, who, as usual, had me laughing at his warm humor. I remembered that he had formerly achieved considerable success as a high school teacher in New York City.

"What a sweet man," I said aloud to my wife.

"And what a perfect honorary president," she remarked.

I reached over to the pen and pad that I kept handy on the end table and wrote a note to Levenson. By the next day, it was typed and in the mail.

"Who knows what could happen?" I thought.

No one was more surprised when the mailman brought me Levenson's reply.

"To be named National Honorary President of Citizens' Scholarship Foundation is the greatest honor I have ever received," he wrote.

"The only problem," Levenson explained, "is that I don't like to travel."

"No problem," I stressed, "What we would like to do is use your name, which is synonymous with education and America."

Levenson invited me, my brother, and our wives to Sardi's in New York for dinner and for more discussion about the goals of Citizens' Scholarship Foundation of America.

He was not only warm and interested, he was also excited about the program. The humorist told us about how all eight children in his family had received their educations at the State University of New York and went on to be artists, doctors and teachers.

"All things are possible in this country," he told us.

It was a marvelous experience. Here we were, dining with one of the most famous personalities of the time -- a man not only deeply concerned about the important matter of education, but informal enough to encourage us to try Sardi's famous desserts -- and then to sample each of ours!

By the end of the meal, we had set a date. Levenson would be installed as the first honorary president of CSFA on January 10, 1961 at a banquet held at Venus de Milo Restaurant in Swansea, Massachusetts. He would accept no payment; we just had to cover his travel expenses.

While Levenson's appointment as president would not begin officially until the night of the dinner, he started working right away. Before heading down to Fall River, Levenson appeared on the Dave Garroway Show on NBC-TV that morning and told his audience about the program.

"The entire community of Fall River should be proud of what has been accomplished," Levenson said, "proud of leading, and more than that, helping the rest of the country."

From New York, he took the train to Providence, where he was a guest on an afternoon television show, filmed two 20-second public service announcements about the Citizens' Scholarship Foundation, then headed into Fall River.

That night at the Venus de Milo Restaurant, more than 400 guests paid $10 to join Levenson for a roast beef dinner and later to listen as the former educator-turned--humorist entertained them with his tales.

First, however, was the business of transforming a local scholarship program into a national foundation. Like its beginnings, the process was kept simple.

Levenson was installed as honorary president, and his first duty was to hand out charters of membership in the national organization to the founding community programs.

Receiving certificates were Raymond Wilson for Fall River, Mass., Mrs. Andrew Jencks for Barrington, R.I., Dr. Charles E. Millard for Warren, R.I., Thomas Keith for Seekonk, Mass., Nathan Isenstadt for Bristol, R.I., Rev. John Elliot for North Kingston, R.I., Amy Connoughton for Dighton-Rehoboth, Mass., John Usher for Berkley--Freetown-Lakeville, Mass., Dr. William Fradkin for Pittsfield, Pennsylvania, and Robert Binkle for Lancaster Pennsylvania.

Although not in attendance, several other communities also joined the new national organization. Receiving certificates were chapters in Covington, Louisiana; Newport News, Virginia; Westerly, Rhode Island; Burlington, New Jersey, and Warren, Rhode Island.

Bringing greetings from the "Scholarship City" was Fall River Mayor John M. Arruda.

"The Fall River Plan is not a panacea for all the ills of American education, but it is a good beginning," he said.

Also paying tribute to the plan and its founders were Superintendent of Schools William S. Lynch, acting director of diocesan schools Rev. Raymond McCarthy, State Senator Mary L. Fonseca, Major Walter P. Parker representing Governor John Volpe, and State Attorney

General Edward J. McCormack. The invocation was given by Rabbi Samuel S. Ruderman and the closing benediction was offered by Rev. Richard S. Hasty.

"We're starting something that is simply grand in the history of the United States," I said. "We've shown the world how a composite of members of a community can work together, without regard to race, creed, or color, with but one thought: to send our deserving young students to higher education.

"While more than 300 to 400 scholarships have been given out in the past year by 20 to 25 communities, the potential growth is amazing."

I remember predicting that, eventually, the scholarships across the country would reach into the millions.

"The beauty of it is that each community is distinct, handling its own students, by itself, solving in its quarter, the educational problem," I told the group. "It is the citizens who do the work from collecting to examining applications to the handing out the cash."

The crowd cheered as Levenson moved to the podium. The comedian hailed me as the "optometrist with vision," a compliment that I would enjoy hearing repeatedly for many years to come.

At first Levenson regaled us with hilarious tales of his humble beginnings and other folksy vignettes; then, he turned serious, commenting on the state of contemporary education.

"We can often forget that what we are trying to do is build a human being. We are trying to help him to develop the gift that God has given him," he said.

And, he noted, for those who are gifted, the response isn't always positive.

"Wouldn't it be wonderful if here in America we greeted a scholarship winner with a brass band like we do acclaimed athletes?" he asked. "The trouble today is that everyone thinks scientists, intellectuals and musicians are 'eggheads.' They think these people are freaks of some sort. In Europe, the intellectuals are acclaimed even by the man on the street."

Levenson lamented the loss of patriotism in the curriculum and culture of the Sixties.

"What we need is more cultural patriotism," he said. "If our primary readers would read, 'America is a free land. America is a good land.' instead of 'John sees the dog. The dog is running.' then perhaps we would be back on the right trail."

After quoting General Omar Bradley, who said, "Americans are nuclear giants but ethical infants," he turned his attention to the potential of Citizens' Scholarship Foundation of America.

"With the scholarship program, we are on the right track," he predicted. "Then we might have the intellectuals taking a real part in the community, coming out of the cushions of their easy chairs to take part in community betterment. We do this by sending all deserving students to college: then they come back to the community and make it a better one."

When Levenson stopped speaking, the applause was deafening. Thomas J. Beedem, who acted as master of ceremonies for the evening, summed up the feelings of the crowd.

"If the people of this area had known what a great time Sam Levenson presented here tonight, there wouldn't be a hall in Fall River that could hold them."

I enjoyed the whole evening. Not only had Levenson really understood that the program could help send young people to college, he saw that it could help reinforce the American values which seemed to be dwindling.

"What a love for America, no, for humanity he has," I remember thinking. "He is an inspiration for us all."

When the bills were paid, Citizens' Scholarship Foundation had made $1,000 on the dinner. We set aside $500 for an essay contest in honor of Sam Levenson which would be open to students in the 11 chapters. Each student addressed the topic: "How I will use my education to build a better America."

The other $500 was used to establish the first national office. For the first time, I, and the other volunteers, no longer had to subsidize the cost of telephone calls and postage for the organization.

Within days, the mail started arriving. Whether from Ringgold, Georgia to Jonesville, Michigan, or from Tyler, Texas to Genesseo, Illinois or Berlin, New Hampshire, they carried pretty much the same message.

"We saw Sam Levenson on the Dave Garroway Show on Tuesday," many said. "Send us material on how we can start a scholarship program."

Some just contained the request; others highlighted the urgent need in their community. We read every one.

"How will we ever answer them all?" I wondered. "It's too wonderful to believe. Thank God for such a man as Sam Levenson; he's really put this program in the hearts of all America."

We brought together volunteers from the private and parochial schools to help with the task of answering all the letters. We sorted the mail and stacked it by state on the ping pong table in my cellar. Within a week, more than 1,200 responses had come from every state in the country. But while the work continued in Fall River, Levenson continued to speak about the program on national television.

When the comedian hosted the Jack Parr Show, I was one of his guests. It was one of the greatest moments of my life. After they put make-up on me.

As I waited backstage for Sam to introduce me to the audience, I was kind of frightened, but I couldn't help thinking, "What a thrill!" And better yet, what an opportunity not only to speak about CSFA to this large audience, but to share the story of democracy in action with the millions of people who watched in homes across the nation.

"The Fall River Plan is a revitalization of the principles and practice of democracy, whereby the means of solving a person's own problems are given to them," I said after being introduced by Levenson.

"They must be made to realize that democracy is not a giveaway," I continued. "It does not mean that the government is going to give them everything. If the government supplies everything, you no longer have a democracy."

Levenson also invited me as his guest when he filled in as Arthur Godfrey's summer replacement on Godfrey's CBS radio show. Before the show, I presented Levenson with a thank you note signed by more than 25,000 citizens' of Fall River. When he saw the size of the scroll, which seemed about the same length as the height of the Empire State building, he was overwhelmed.

"You're kidding," Levenson said to me. "You don't always get a chance to help your country -- don't let it slip through your fingers."

During the show, the audience was attentive and seemed to be genuinely interested. They weren't the only ones who cared about the program. After the show, even the musicians, producers and engineers stopped to question me about starting similar plans. The Four Amigos, a quartet from Puerto Rico, was also curious about the international possibilities.

Back home, requests from television viewers and radio listeners continued to arrive, many simply addressed to "The Fall River Plan." By the end of January, we had received more than 2,500 letters.

The noted comedian Steve Allen sent in $100, and he provided no address so we couldn't even contact him to say thank you. Hugh Downs also was interested and even became a member of the board.

As news of the program spread from coast to coast, in Fall River, there was paper work to be done. Mrs. Doris Cooper, a Fall River housewife, was chosen secretary and became the organization's first paid employee. Her office space and equipment were contributed by Philip Goltz, a Fall River attorney.

As the news about Citizens' Scholarship Foundation spread, there were more and more requests for me to speak. I always tried to schedule them for Tuesday night or Wednesday, which was my day off.

Sometimes, patients would complain. Many said, "He's too busy with his scholarship program to bother with us."

Even though I tried to take care of the vision needs of my patients, I still had the need to share my larger vision of America. I would try to explain how motivating students and supplying them with scholarship money would give them access to higher education. Since the foundation of our democracy is based upon education, a better educated populace logically would strengthen our country.

But while the work I did for CSFA was indeed a great sacrifice, especially when I was trying to build a practice, it also provided me with some wonderful moments.

One day, while I was in Rhode Island speaking, Fred Margolis called with some incredible news.

"Irving," he said, "we just got a package. Are you sitting down? It contains $1,440."

I was flabbergasted -- and concerned that the money had been gotten illegally. We called the FBI and the local police departments. They had no report of missing money, and said it was ours to keep.

Just to be sure, we contacted the Associated Press and United Press International. Newspapers all over the country headlined the story: "Christmas Came Early."

Six months later, we received another package with $1,600, and three months later, another with $2,000. Like the first, they all contained the note which said, "For your scholarship program."

Only one had an address in Phoenix, Arizona. When we called, the listing was for a vacant lot. Whoever the donor was, we never found out. The person had a lot of faith in me to trust me with that kind of an anonymous gift.

Another time, we received three $100 bills. The only address was Buffalo, New York.

The fact that people were willing to contribute gave me further inspiration, and I continued my trips to speak before as many community gatherings as possible.

Although I traveled all over this country, the trips were not very enjoyable. I really only saw airports and banquet halls. Even the friends I met were not lasting relationships because of the physical distance that separated us.

As I went from town to town, I was sometimes described as "Johnny Appleseed." I guess I was a little like him. I dropped off the seeds of the program but never was able to see them grow and mature.

Often I would stress that one of the great challenges that exists in this country today is whether or not the citizens of America understand democracy sufficiently to assume their rightful responsibility and leadership to fulfill this dream of democracy. Then, as now, democracy is still on trial, and the dream can only be fulfilled by educating our young people.

While Americans have always enjoyed the benefits of democracy, they have to be willing to assume the responsibility of leadership by example. That is what Citizens' Scholarship Foundation is really about. It provides access to education, as well as an example of democracy in action.

"We are trying to breathe new meaning and reason for education," I said to a group in Lancaster, Pennsylvania. "An education in a democracy is not enough; what is also needed is the willingness to share knowledge and yourself with your fellow man by participating in the political, cultural and civic life of your community."

"CSF believes in the dream of America. It believes that the American citizens, when properly motivated and inspired, will be willing to assume the leadership and responsibility in the attempt to provide higher education, skill and knowledge to perpetuate our form of government for our most valued and priceless asset our country possesses, our young children."

Although the message I gave to the Lancaster group was important, the thing I remember most was how we got there.

Bill McGee, who often served as the official CSF photographer, went with me one Sunday morning for a three-day trip to Amish country.

We arrived at the Eastern Air Lines terminal with some time to spare and Bill dropped a few quarters into one of the machines that sell life insurance. Without much thought, he signed his wife's name on the policy and we boarded flight 621.

The plane's propellers began spinning and smoking as we lifted off promptly at 8:15 in the morning. Before long, we had to land at Idlewild, New Jersey because a snow storm was sweeping up the coast. Because all connecting flights were canceled, we had to take a bus to a helicopter. After 20 minutes, we landed at the Newark, New Jersey airport.

It was there that we learned our flight out of Newark was canceled because of bad weather. The woman at the desk gave us a refund and a ticket for a taxi ride to Penn Station. The snow kept on coming.

At noon we arrived at Penn Station and waited an hour for the train. The luggage and long walk slowed me down, but neither inconvenience nor weather would stop me from sharing the Fall River Plan with the good people of Lancaster who were being blanketed with four inches of snow as we waited.

When the train arrived, we walked to the farthest car, but still couldn't find a seat. We stood in the aisle, sometimes taking a break by sitting on our luggage. Because we were headed directly into the storm, the trip took longer than expected, and we arrived in Philadelphia about an hour late.

At least in Philadelphia we were able to get seats, and we settled in for the ride to Lancaster. When we finally arrived, we were met by Robert Binkle of the Kiwanis Club. By the time we reached the hotel, it was 5:30.

The meeting started at 6:00, and we were there, a little weary from the trip, but full of enthusiasm. Because of the weather, only 35 of the 150 expected were present, but they decided to form a chapter. Our often challenging trip had been worth it.

Trips like these were not only hard on me, but also trying for my family. My wife was not comfortable alone with our young children, so she kept the lights on when I was away. To make matters worse, whenever I was not at home, Charlotte just could not bring herself to sleep in our bed alone. I felt guilty knowing that she never did get a good night's sleep on the couch.

Yet, through it all, she was supportive and never asked me to stop. She also saw the potential of CSF and believed that we could help make the country better.

As I told the group in Lancaster and elsewhere, these young people need to receive concrete and positive examples of the local community willing to sacrifice to help them. If I asked them to sacrifice, then as the president of the Foundation, I had to do so as well.

Actually, I was happy to travel to Iowa, Florida, California and other states spreading the news about the Citizens' Scholarship Foundation, but my practice and family life were feeling the strain. As early as 1961,I realized that we needed to put together a permanent office staff if we were going to succeed.

One of the first steps in making that happen was taken when I told the CSFA story to Senator Everett Saltonstall. Although I had never met him, I made it a point to look him up when I was in Washington, D.C. I felt that, as the senior Senator from my state, he should know about Citizens' Scholarship Foundation.

He was wonderful. Not only did he agree to meet with me, but he had the story of CSFA entered in the Congressional Record. He also suggested that I contact the Ford Foundation for information about grants.

"What Chutzpah!" I thought as I dared to call on Alvin Eurich, president of the Ford Foundation Fund for the Advancement of Education.

He thought the program was worthy of help and suggested that I meet Roy Larsen, the chairman of the board.

Here was one of the most powerful and prestigious men in America, and he was willing to meet with me and to offer his help. Although I was honored and surprised, I found over the years that oftentimes the most powerful people are also the ones who understand that the challenge of democracy is that we help one another. Larsen was such a man.

In his spacious office in the Time-Life Building, Larsen not only listened to my plea, but wrote us a check for $12,000 from his discretionary account.

He explained he could write out an award for up to $15,000 without board approval, and we deserved the help. I knew there and then that we were on the road to success.

"Every time that we try to lift a problem from our own shoulders and shift that problem to the hands of the government, to the same extent, we are sacrificing the liberties of the people."

- John F. Kennedy

CHAPTER 6
THE FOUNDATION IS SET

On May 15, 1961, we officially incorporated Citizens' Scholarship Foundation of America. For the first time in its history, thanks to the Ford Foundation grant, we had some money to work with. I decided that I was not an administrator, and if we were to grow, we had to grow with a professional at the helm.

Many people have asked me why I would start an organization and then not accept a paid position. I would have loved to serve as director, but I also know my limitations. So we hired Fred Margolis as our first full-time executive director, and I remained the unpaid president.

While the finances allowed us to set up an office, it also gave us some credibility as an organization, as did more appearances on television and radio shows, as well as articles in *Reader's Digest*, *Time*, and the *Saturday Review*, among other national publications.

CSF chapters organized in Urbandale, Iowa; Vero Beach, Florida; North Charlestown, South Carolina; Claremont, New Hampshire; and Wappingers Falls, New York. In each community, despite its different needs, the program worked.

In addition to the Ford Foundation grant, other organizations saw the benefits of providing seed money to our fledgling group. The Spaulding-Potter Charitable Fund in New Hampshire, the Kettering Foundation in Ohio and the Lilly Endowment in Indiana all helped to stimulate thousands of new dollars at the local chapter level.

The grants also allowed me to travel greater distances to speak to groups and to welcome them into CSFA. For the first time, some of my expenses were covered.

It was a good thing, because my practice was beginning to suffer as patients called and found that I was out of town once again. The real estate that I had purchased and left with a partner to manage was lost. To say the least, I was getting discouraged.

Looking back, I figured out that those 18 houses would have generated enough income and increased in value to the point where I would have become a millionaire. I gave up and lost a lot because of CSFA, but the struggle was worth it when I watched the dream evolve and spread across the country.

Things weren't much easier for the Foundation. In fact, from 1963 to 1971, it was often a battle just to survive. What helped CSFA along were state and regional development projects and grants from such corporations as Time, S & H Foundation, Carling Brewing Company, and General Electric.

These unrestricted funds allowed us to maintain an office which we located at 43 Leon Street in Boston. The small paid staff developed such services as blanket tax rulings, campaign materials, promotional items and chapter manuals.

I finally felt we were on our way. Despite the help from the staff, I continued to travel and speak out for the program but remained unsalaried.

Out of curiosity, I decided to keep track of my travels in 1964. From January to April, I attended 45 meetings or speeches taking me from Boston to California with stops in Michigan, Colorado, and Kansas (See Appendix F for the complete list).

Wherever I went, I was constantly asked the same questions:

"What's in it for you?"

"What's the gimmick?"

"What's in it for me? A lot," I'd respond. "If you can give young people a better future; if you can help them become better citizens, and commit themselves to giving something back to America, then I will benefit -- you will benefit -- our children will benefit -- and our grandchildren will benefit by continuing and nourishing this great experiment called democracy."

At our new home office in Boston, we elected Eugene Struckhoff as chairman. Struckhoff, a New Hampshire lawyer and trust administrator who later became President of the Council on Foundations and a nationally recognized expert in the community foundation field. He provided CSFA with more of a structure and wrote the by-laws that basically still govern the organization today. But more importantly, he brought quality people to the board and developed the idea of incentive grants.

For the first time, with the help of a $40,000 Spaulding Potter Charitable Fund grant, CSFA had the resources for the organization to challenge communities to start their own program by offering to match funds raised in each locality. This resulted in 44 new chapters in New Hampshire.

After seeing the success in New Hampshire, the Kettering Foundation, in 1964, provided $75,000 for work in Ohio and a $65,000 grant from the Lilly Endowment helped spread the work in Indiana.

While I was thrilled with the success of the Foundation, and happy to travel across the country sharing just how people could keep the spirit of democracy alive through CSF, I learned a lesson about priorities in 1967.

While on a speaking engagement in Erie, Pennsylvania, I called home, fully expecting to find my youngest son Russ home from the hospital in Boston following some routine tests. Instead, I was told to head right for the hospital from the airport.

It seems complications had set in. At the hospital, I found him in critical condition, with tubes all over him.

I was devastated! I vowed never to leave my family again for any reason.

Thank God, the doctors were able to correct the problem, but it took me a long time to get over the guilt of being far away and out of reach while my son was close to death. In fact, it took a lot of convincing by my wife to assure me that everything was now okay at home, and that I should continue with my mission.

There was also good news for CSFA in 1967, when William Norris was elected chairman of the board, and, in 1968, when Joseph F. Phelan was hired as executive director. Joe brought greater administrative strength and stability to the organization.

Hiring an executive director can often make or break an organization, and I was happy to hear that Joe Phelan would lead CSFA. Joe had a Master's Degree, and he had taught English at Bristol High School in New Hampshire. While at the school, he had directed the CSFA Youth Branch, then had gone on to be director of the program in New Hampshire and Maine.

"This is wonderful," I thought. "He is already well versed in the operation of CSFA. We are fortunate to have him."

There's a delicate balance in running a non-profit organization. Making money can easily become too big of a priority. Joe kept the dream of CSFA alive by focusing on the people who are the backbone and strength of the program.

Meanwhile, my hip had been deteriorating over the years, and it gave me so much trouble that the doctors replaced it with a cup in 1969. That was not very successful, so in 1970 I had my first total hip replacement.

Still, I continued to travel, using crutches or a cane to get along. Many people thought I was crazy to travel and speak in my condition, but I had to. Throughout my journeys I met so many marvelous people who were so dedicated and interested in helping others. I had to go, and when I did, it proved to me that the dream of democracy was still alive and well in the Citizens' Scholarship Foundation.

It also became clear to me that even though corporate and financial support for CSFA increased, it could not keep pace with the increasing costs of maintaining a national organization.

Edward Lee, a Westfield, Massachusetts attorney, was elected chairman of the board in 1971. I was happy to see him in the position. We had originally met in 1962 when he became the first campaign chairman for the newly formed Westfield chapter.

No one could see what his impact would be, but he told me that his personal objective was to develop a reliable annual base of income for the national program, thus allowing the grants to be used for special development projects.

"So be it," I thought, but then again, I never was one for finances.

In their capable hands, Lee and Phelan moved the CSFA office to Concord, New Hampshire, and together they began administering scholarships for the New Hampshire Charitable Fund in 1971.

This was a big move for us. By administering this plan, we had shown that CSFA could apply the concepts and procedures of the community scholarship plan to other funds. By 1973, CSFA was awarding grants for five separate funds totaling $42,000.

I was really excited about the concept and its success, but I continued to focus on chapters. I would visit the chapters and explain to them how they could keep alive the spirit of democracy.

Over the years, my association with CSFA has brought me in contact with many well-known individuals and in the mid-1970s, Joe Phelan and I were invited to the home of DeWitt Wallace, the founder of *Reader's Digest*.

What a pleasure and honor it was to meet with him and enjoy lunch at his home. Over the years, I have always considered Wallace and his magazine the "godfather" of CSF, because the original article in 1962 helped spread the story about the program throughout the country.

Wallace and the Reader's Digest Foundation also provided an incentive grant to encourage 15 exemplary chapters with a $500 Reader's Digest Scholarship. This further encouraged the spread and growth of CSF.

The real turning point for CSFA, I think, came in 1976 when Humphrey Doermann, president of the Bush Foundation, granted $140,000 plus $60,000 three years later to expand the program in Minnesota. With those grants, Marlys and Stuart Johnson were hired to develop the program there.

As part of their campaign to spread the word in Minnesota, the Johnsons ran state-wide workshops, and they asked me to speak at one of the conferences. A week before the program, I hydroplaned off an icy highway and Charl broke her leg.

I felt torn. Here was my wife at home in a cast and needing a walker to help her move around the house. But a lot depended on how the program worked in Minnesota, and people were planning to travel as much as eight hours or more to hear me speak.

"Go," Charl insisted. "I have friends all around. I'll be all right."

That's the kind of support I had, and still have, at home. Even though she hated to be alone, and I can't stand sleeping by myself in a hotel room, we both wanted the program to succeed. And so I went to Minnesota, and the convention was a success. When I returned to my wife's loving arms, everything there was fine as well.

Under the spirited, innovative and dedicated leadership of the Johnsons, CSFA was instrumental in expanding the Minnesota program. In fact, from 1976 to 1991, the $200,000 Bush Foundation grants eventually generated an unbelievable total of $37 million in scholarships from Minnesota communities and corporations.

That's not only an unbeatable record, but what a wonderful way for a Foundation to inaugurate an idea! And the 1976 Bicentennial year was not over yet.

The same year, the Toro Company became CSFA's first corporate client, and, again, CSFA proved that the same principles which guided our work in the communities could be applied successfully to corporations that wanted to offer scholarships to employees, customers and other selected groups.

In a way the project with Toro changed the whole concept of CSFA. David McLaughlin, President of Toro, and later President of Dartmouth College and the Aspen Institute, said, "We don't want to be involved in deciding which applicants get the scholarships. We trust your expertise and integrity."

Non-profit organizations can't survive without a reliable source of funds, and finally, thanks to the initiative of Joe Phelan and Ed Lee, CSFA had found a way to generate revenue without draining finances from the communities. In fact, today a portion of the money earned by servicing corporations continues to allow CSFA to help new chapters start and support existing ones.

Financially, starting a chapter is a losing financial proposition because servicing the chapters costs more than the dues they pay. CSFA has always felt that the scholarship money raised by each community should be kept and awarded in each community. In the long run, the money spent by CSFA and the scholarships awarded by each community are investments, because the health and strength of America lies in developing better Americans. By helping provide educational opportunities, CSFA is really investing in the future.

In addition to helping more young people through administering the corporate scholarships, CSFA also found a way to become self-sufficient. For managing each corporate-sponsored scholarship program, CSFA was able to charge a small service fee. But CSFA has also helped the corporations significantly because the organization has a way to process applications fairly and efficiently, while responding to the interests and needs of corporations with flexibility and quality of service.

This partnership between CSFA and the corporations was a marvelous idea, and by the way, one with which I had nothing to do. It also is an example of how CSFA is a program that allows people to take a basic idea and expand it. In every community we go to, people say, "Hey, why don't we do it that way."

CSFA also provides an opportunity for learning to work with people and organizations. In fact many people have taken the lessons learned by developing chapters and applied them by creating grass-roots efforts to build playgrounds, pools, or other projects in their own communities.

In fact, I did it myself. Back home in Fall River, I co-founded the Interfaith Council in 1978. Thanks to CSF, I had developed some credibility with the local media, and the Council grew out of the reputation we had of not discriminating against any group and crossing all lines.

Our first project as an Interfaith Council was a dinner featuring the noted Polish Roman Catholic priest, Rev. Robert S. Kaczynski, as the speaker on the scheduled day in November. The weather was horrible, and the media warned people to stay off the snowy streets. Although people had told me that if we sold 75 tickets we would be successful, we sold 700 tickets by selling tables to various groups and organizations.

The management of Venus de Milo Restaurant said they would not hold us to the minimum we guaranteed. Lo and behold, 700 people showed up. Father K. did a great job and everybody felt so good that annually we are able to launch a Brotherhood-Sisterhood Dinner, and usually we average 500 to 600 people.

It was so marvelous to see tables of Catholics, Protestants, along with Orthodox and Conservative Jews together. When they all got up to sing "Let There Be Peace on Earth" and "God Bless America," it was awesome.

Through the Interfaith Council we have tackled a great many issues. One was domestic violence. Sergeant Richard Levesque, a police officer friend, told me about how domestic violence constitutes the greatest abuse against women and children, and I said the only thing we can do is give it coverage.

We decided to sponsor a panel discussion with professionals telling why domestic abuse is detrimental to the community and a blot on American society. This forum provided an opportunity to help rectify a problem.

The Council provided a neutral platform to be able to talk and to meet on issues that concerned us all. I think the Interfaith Council has been a very, very good thing, because it is another way to show community residents just how fortunate they are to live in America.

We also hosted the program for Martin Luther King Jr. Day after the retirement of Judge Thomas Quinn who had started the program. It's a necessity to show that all races can and have contributed to America. The more you give people a chance to be recognized as Americans, the more you treat them as equals, the more they will contribute to society and the stronger the community and our country will be.

That's one of the great things about Martin Luther King Day. It points out that everybody has a God-given talent to contribute to our country.

Another annual event, the Holocaust Program was also begun about the same time. Each year guest speakers help us recall and learn from the lessons of the maltreatment and murder of six million Jews during the Nazi era. At first people questioned the benefit of holding such an event. What happened was so horrible, they said, why should we want to talk about it.

"You know," I told the audience who attended the first year's program, "what happened elsewhere is possible here and if you do not understand history, it has been said, then you are bound to repeat it. And I don't ever want to see it happen in this country."

Again, I was told if you have 50 people the first year, it will be a success. We had an overflow crowd at Bristol Community College.

Since then we have run the program in churches, colleges, but most importantly in a court house. That's significant because the Nazis took over the judicial system, and that's how they were able to do what they did. By having the program in a court room, we drew attention to the fact that we can never allow the horrors of Holocaust to happen in this country.

Although America is the greatest country in the world, we have to take responsibility for it or someone may come along and say, "I'm going to usurp this power and I'm going to subjugate you in time to come." This must never come to pass.

Even though the Interfaith Council and the other programs I've been involved in do not deal directly with the main subject of this book -- providing hope and encouragement through scholarships -- they are part of my dream of a better America, based on understanding, respect and cooperation with one another. Education is necessary, but education can only flourish when people of all faiths and persuasions can come together in peace and harmony to work for the betterment of their entire communities.

"So, then, to every man his chance -- to every man, regardless of his birth, his shining, golden opportunity --to every man his right to live, to work, to be himself, and to become whatever thing his manhood and his vision can combine to make him -- this, seeker, is the promise of America."

- *Thomas Wolfe*

CHAPTER 7
THE COUNTRY RESPONDS

As the seventies came to a close, CSFA continued to grow. In 1978, Jostens, a school ring and yearbook publishing company, presented CSFA with its first national challenge when they asked the Foundation to administer its nationwide scholarship competition.

Again, the Foundation was up to the challenge. It brought together applications from students all over the United States, and with the same fairness and impartiality, helped Jostens recognize outstanding high school students through the Jostens Leaders program.

Ralph H. Seifert, an insurance agency executive and old friend and chapter president from Mansfield, Mass., was elected chairman of the Board in 1979. He was a spark plug and a dynamo who immediately made it his mission to restructure CSFA in a much more business-like fashion.

While I agreed that this had to be done, I also felt that I needed to step down as permanent president in order to let CSFA grow. Executive Director Joseph F. Phelan was named president in 1980.

Still, by virtue of my title of Founder, I continued to travel to board meetings and visit with chapters. I was in constant touch with the officers because I didn't want the basic goal of the program to change as CSFA grew.

The ideal time to re-focus on the principles of CSFA came in 1982, when we celebrated the 25th Anniversary of the beginning of the first Dollars for Scholars chapter in Fall River.

I could hardly believe it. Citizens' Scholarship Foundation was truly a national organization, and when I went to local chapter presentations, at times I saw the children of some of our first recipients receiving awards.

To honor CSFA's outstanding chapter volunteers, the Board of Directors established the National Honor Roll. What a great opportunity that was to have the people who worked so hard without remuneration recognized in this way by their own chapters -- and what better way to keep tapping their resources for inspiration and knowledge. Today over 100 volunteers have been recognized for outstanding service to their local Dollars for Scholars chapters.

Just as corporations found a partner in CSFA, universities and colleges joined together with the Foundation in providing assistance to students. The Collegiate Partners Program was established in 1984, and with it another dream of mine came true. I had always felt that colleges should be willing to match grants awarded to students, and this was now coming to be.

Like many aspects of CSFA, the colleges got involved almost by chance. I was at a program honoring Martin Luther King, Jr. at the Bristol District Court House in Fall River when I met Dr. Richard A. Boudreau, president of Fisher Junior College. When I started to tell him about the program, he stopped me.

"You don't have to tell me about CSF. My wife was a recipient," he said.

He not only thought my idea of colleges matching grants received by students was worthwhile, right there and then he committed himself to setting up a program at Fisher which would match any of our scholarships up to $500 at any of the school's campuses in Massachusetts.

As the Collegiate Partners, Dollars for Scholars, and Scholarship Management Services of CSFA expanded, the need for a new headquarters also became apparent. To my astonishment, new headquarters were funded, constructed and occupied in St. Peter, Minnesota. The Board decided to move the organization's headquarters to Minnesota to be more in the middle of the country.

"I personally am amazed, overwhelmed and flabbergasted that an unknown, with no money -- an ordinary citizen with a dream -- can see this magnificent edifice become a reality," I admitted at the dedication of the new headquarters building, a beautiful New England style office building overlooking the Minnesota River Valley in St. Peter.

In a way, however, I saw the completion of a national headquarters building as an affirmation of all I believed.

"If you will it and are willing to sacrifice and work long hours, it can be realized -- but only in our democracy, our America," I said.

What a long way we had come from setting up an office on a ping-pong table in a basement, to shared space, to a real office and now to a beautiful, new building in the heartland of America.

CSFA continued to expand its services to many more communities and to corporations like Burger King and Chrysler. Regional offices were opened in Southern California, in Wakefield, Massachusetts, and in other regions as new chairman Burt Knauft, Executive Vice President of Independent Sector, worked to develop the board and the organization.

After a brilliant regime which left CSFA in a stable financial position with a most productive and dedicated board and staff, Joseph F. Phelan resigned in 1986. The organization was now ready to move on from a solid plateau to even greater heights under the next president.

After a nation-wide search, Dr. William C. Nelsen was hired as the new CSFA executive officer. When Bill was hired, he was the immediate past president of Augustana College in South Dakota and had previously served as Vice President of St. Olaf College and as Program Executive with the Danforth Foundation.

"What a fine man," I thought. "He will continue to bring this program to people throughout the country."

Under his leadership, CSFA has expanded rapidly. Regional offices for the Dollars for Scholars Program have opened and/or expanded in Minnesota, North Dakota, the Pacific Northwest, California, New York, New England, Indiana, and Baltimore. Student Aid Management Services marketing offices have also been opened in Connecticut, Virginia, and Georgia.

While staying true to the mission, Bill and CSFA have worked to spread the program to more and more people. By 1993 the number of Collegiate Partners had grown to almost 300, the number of chapters reached 650, and the number of corporate clients expanded to 450. Each of these figures has more than doubled in the past six years!

Under President Nelsen's leadership, CSFA has focussed in recent years not only on towns and rural areas but increasingly in helping disadvantaged students in inner-city areas. Some new programs go beyond awarding student aid to assisting and motivating students to learn and achieve.

The Pepsi School Challenge program is one example of how the Foundation has worked with inner-city schools in

Detroit, Dallas and elsewhere. The Pepsi Cola Company offers $250 each semester to every student who meets state attendance records, maintains a C average and stays drug free. Those who succeed receive $2,000 toward college or vocational training.

The Pepsi School Challenge has been an incredible success! In Dallas, during the first year, participating students outperformed nonparticipants by 22 percent. In the second year, 83 percent of the students achieved a 2.0 GPA or above. Students seeking post-secondary education increased by 79 percent and the overall dropout rate declined by 40 percent.

As Dr. Nelsen has noted, the Pepsi School Challenge in Dallas and Detroit is an excellent example of what can happen when we say to students: "You are important. You have talents to do well, and we will challenge you and assist you." But then again, that has been the message of CSFA right from the beginning. I am also so glad to see that many new Dollars for Scholars chapters are now being formed in inner-city areas.

Volunteers have also continued to give great leadership to CSFA. From 1988 to 1992, Lloyd Brandt, former President of the First Bank System's Foundation, served with great dedication as Chair of the Board and in Fall, 1992, John Wedum, a Midwest and Florida businessman, with great entrepreneurial skills became Board Chair.

CSFA's successes and my commitment to the program have led to my receiving many awards, citations and keys to various cities, but the best and greatest tribute is that the dream of Citizens' Scholarship Foundation remains alive. Despite the growth, despite the moves, despite the changes in personnel, CSFA remains committed to the same goals we set in Fall River back in 1958.

While the program was thriving, I had a personal set-back in 1988 when I had a heart attack. Fortunately, the medication TPA was available, and the doctors were able to dissolve a dangerous blood clot.

After a few days in intensive care, a nurse stopped by. She didn't look familiar, yet she seemed to know me.

"Dr. Fradkin," she said, "you don't know me, I'm Pauline De Mello Sardinha. I was the second oldest of eight children and never would have been able to become a nurse if I hadn't received help from Citizens' Scholarship Foundation.

"I hadn't really expected to receive any money, but I became a recipient of one of those scholarships in 1965, and the money covered all my expenses for three years at Truesdale Hospital. That money gave me my start for a prosperous and rewarding career in nursing."

It was ironic that my recovery was helped along by Sardinha's tender loving care. It was as gratifying to know that she was a CSF recipient.

Two years later, we met again when her daughter Kerry received a scholarship from the Somerset, Massachusetts chapter and again in 1991, when her son Kevin received a scholarship.

Once again in 1992 I was in the hospital for my third hip replacement. As always I continued to tell people about CSF, and sometimes good things came from my conversations.

The head nurse at the hospital not only listened to me, but she became a CSF volunteer. She also helped convince the New England Baptist Nursing School to set aside money to establish two scholarships for minority nursing students in the new Dudley Street Dollars for Scholars Chapter, based in Boston, Massachusetts.

New England received its own regional office that same year with a staff and resources geared to expanding the program in the very region where it started, thanks to Dr. Nelsen's expert direction, active volunteer work by Board member Joe Hinchey, Senior Vice President of Analog Devices, and contributions from New England corporations and foundations. I, of course, continue to help in any way possible, especially in communities throughout the New England area.

In a way, we had come full-circle. Despite the recession, during its 30th anniversary year CSFA awarded a total of $25 million to almost 28,000 students. After three decades, the need is still there; in fact, it has become greater.

An editorial in the *Fall River Herald News* noted:

"This year no one needs to be told that money is tighter than it has been in a decade. Economic problems are pressing for almost everyone. Meanwhile, education costs more than ever. The need young students have for funds is especially great as a result."

Ironically, the passage was a quote from a 1971 editorial. We have come so far, yet we still have so far to go. With the help of every American citizen, we can realize the dream.

"People should come here to create a better society rather than to make a better living. The Founding Fathers did not create a land of opportunists, they created a land of opportunity. We are not going to eliminate selfishness. That's not what I'm advocating. But we must show that in the long run the welfare of America is also their own welfare, and that of their children,and great-grandchildren."

- *Vartan Gregorian, President, Brown University*

CHAPTER 8
THE DREAM CONTINUES THROUGH COMMUNITIES, COLLEGES, AND COMPANIES

Focusing on the Chapters

Even though the Citizens' Scholarship Foundation of America has grown incredibly over the years, the chapters remain the most important part of the program. There have been amazing results in the communities; they provide proof positive that people will support their own.

In each of the past four years, the number of chapters has increased by almost 100, in part because of the hard work of dedicated people who have realized that they do not merely have a job -- they have a mission. Together with countless volunteers, CSFA staff helps keep the dream of CSFA alive.

The program has grown and grown, to a great extent thanks to the efforts of staff members like Mary Adams Forsberg, National Director, and Betty Torgerson, National Coordinator for Dollars for Scholars; Nancy Caldwell Mead, Senior Area Director and James Pritchett, Urban Initiative Director for the Great Lakes Region; Julie

Scullard, former Area Director and Peg Ward, current Area Director for the Mid-Atlantic Region; Curtis V. Trygstad, Area Director and John Nadeau, former Area Director for the Midwest Region; Sally Evers Woodyard, Area Director for the Pacific Northwest Region; Alison Velez' Lane, Area Director for Baltimore; Stephen M. Pratt, Area Director for the New England Region; and several Area Directors for California.

Across the nation, the programs and services offered by Citizens' Scholarship Foundation of America have been accepted and welcomed by hundreds of communities. The proof of the program's success can be found in the patchwork of neighborhoods that have made CSFA their own. From small farming communities to large urban communities, from poor inner-city minority communities to rich, suburban communities, Citizens' Scholarship Foundation of America has been accepted and used as a model to help young people.

The willingness of people of all colors, religions, and economic backgrounds to voluntarily help each other is as pure an American tradition as anything. As Vartan Gregorian and others have suggested, I don't think there's another country in the world where people are willing to give of themselves the way Americans do -- if properly motivated and stimulated.

No other country that I know of has a system of financial aid which comes from the people. England, Poland and other European countries will give scholarships, but the awards come almost exclusively from the government, not the people. In most countries, the government will make scholarships available to individuals. They make the awards because they realize, and rightly so, that there will be tremendous problems in a country that does not have quality education. Most successful governments have learned that you cannot develop your country if you do not have your people educated.

Even in America, where education has been part of the foundation of our democracy since it began, there remains a tremendous need for programs like Citizens' Scholarship Foundation of America which are dedicated to helping educate youth.

It isn't hard to find articles in just about any newspaper which paint a depressing picture of contemporary education in this country.

The Census Bureau reported in a June, 1992 Associated Press story that 40 percent of boys and 29 percent of girls ages 15 to 17 were either one or more grades behind in school or had left school without graduating. They went on to note that more minorities and economically challenged youngsters either fall behind or drop out of school.

Forbes Magazine produced a special supplement on education in 1988, in cooperation with CSFA, that focused on the crisis in education. It suggested that one-fourth of all ninth graders will fail to finish high school, that too many students have limited access and choice when it comes to higher education, and that high school graduates face rising costs for post-secondary education. In 1993 the picture has hardly improved:

· The high school drop out rate remains at close to 29 percent nationwide and more than 50 percent in some urban areas.

· Proficiency in literacy, math, and science among U.S. students has declined compared to students in other industrialized countries.

· Fewer minorities and economically disadvantaged youths are going to college, and of those who attend college, many do not graduate.

·Higher education costs have increased dramatically -- by the year 2000, four years of post-secondary education are projected to reach $51,000 at a public college and $109,000 at a private college.

Way back in 1959, I thought that education was coming to the point where only the wealthy would be going to private schools. "This is really getting out of hand," I thought.

In 1993, things are worse than I thought then. The cost of higher education has increased so dramatically that it's becoming a rich man's game. That's to the detriment of our country.

I do not believe this country will survive if only the rich go to private schools and the working class sons and daughters go to public schools. There should be a mix. People should get to know one another. They've got to work with one another -- that is the whole future and the basis of continued success of our democracy.

The concerns and resources of individual communities must be marshaled in a cost-effective manner to encourage students to do well in elementary and high schools, to pursue post-secondary education, and to make contributions in their personal lives and careers. This is the reason why scholarships in particular are so important.

As I've said time and time again, providing financial aid is a pure American idea. The concept of people voluntarily coming forth and making money available so that the young people, the future leaders of their communities, can be helped toward a better education is an example of democracy in action.

Scholarships permit a donor to play a small role in the lives of individuals without assuming the entire financial responsibility for the student's success. Scholarship express confidence in the recipient and let them know that someone cares.

That feeling of support is so important in a young person's life. As our youth develop, they need to know that people care. A great way for adults in a community to help and to demonstrate concern is to provide scholarships.

A scholarship is a gift, however, that is gratefully returned. We have seen, over the years, that students receiving scholarships from the people in the community not only feel that they have more of an obligation to do well in school, but also that they usually repay the scholarships back when and if they are able either through financial gifts or volunteer service -- or both!

Scholarships, though generally modest in size, touch many on the way to serving a great purpose. From the student and the parent, to the high school and the college, scholarships generate excitement for everyone concerned.

And they do create excitement! Just the thought of anyone saying "Hey, we can work together -- we can make this possible" makes a community come together. In doing so, the future leaders of our community, of our country, are not only going to get an education, they are going to remember that it was the people in their city or town who worked together to make their education possible.

It is a forward-looking community that helps its young people. When people come together with gifts, ranging from as small as one dollar to as large as a hundred or a thousand dollars, they show that they are willing to express confidence in the next generation. These communities are providing for the educational future of their own natural resources -- their young people.

But there are many who do not see scholarships as an investment. According to a study by the College Board, in relation to increased college costs, financial aid for students actually declined more than 14 percent in the Eighties. We must reverse this trend!

Even those groups who do award scholarships have not kept up with the economic realities. The relative dollar value of the scholarships declines as college costs increase.

We, at Citizens' Scholarship Foundation of America, constantly urge our chapters to increase the dollar amounts of their scholarships. The average dollar amount today varies from $500 to $1,500, although some chapters are able to award much larger scholarships. Although five or six hundred dollars may not seem like a lot of money, if you put that amount toward a state school which only costs, at the present time in many states, about $2,000 or so a year, that's 25 percent of the cost and a tremendous help. Although $1,500 may not seem like much when going to more expensive schools, when put together with other financial aid, the award opens up new choices and opportunities for a student.

Scholarships also help cut down or eliminate the need for student loans. With private school costs doubling and public school tuition increasing nearly 81 percent over the past ten years, according to the College Board, more students are borrowing but even more are finding it difficult to repay their debts. Recently, A. Dallas Martin, Jr., president of the National Association of Student Financial Aid Administrators, was quoted in an Associated Press article as explaining that parents are finding it difficult to keep up with student loans, and that the tight job market forces more students to default on loans.

With CSFA and Dollars for Scholars community support, an education is still possible. If we the free people say, "This is my responsibility;" we can do it. And, more importantly, if those receiving scholarships say, "I have been helped. I want to in turn help somebody else," then our future is almost insured.

For those who have been helped by CSFA, the benefits are obvious, but to other groups, the rewards are also many. CSFA offers just so many reasons to become a part of it. In our program, we currently ask only $100 a year dues, and many times a service club or bank will pick up the dues. If they cover the administrative fee, then 100 percent of all the money raised by a chapter stays in the local community to help local youth!

And for $100 what is it that CSFA will do for you? By virtue of affiliation with CSFA, a community receives many valuable materials and services including:

· The Dollars for Scholars Guides to Chapter Operations, Chapter Publicity, Fund Raising, Awards, and Academic Support Activities.

· The use of CSFA tax rulings, including nonprofit and public foundation status.

· The use of all CSFA trademarks, including the mortarboard/book logo, Citizens' Scholarship Foundation of America® and Dollars for Scholars®.

· The use of all CSFA Dollars for Scholars materials including promotional and fund raising items at low cost.

· The use of all CSFA financial services including filing of IRS reports.

· Access to CSFA's Chapter Investment Pool.

· Access to CSFA-sponsored Community Volunteer Service Awards.

Chuck Rickett, former general manager of the Hartford City News Times, Inc. in Indiana and former volunteer director of the Blackford County Chapter of CSFA said it well when he noted:

"Each CSFA Dollars for Scholars chapter operates its program independently, adopting and adapting CSFA chapter operations, services, and materials to meet community needs. In every instance, however, volunteers respond to the needs of qualified students going on to two- and four-year colleges, universities, and vocational-technical schools.

"Even if your city or town currently supports a community-wide scholarship activity, CSFA has something of value to lend to your program. CSFA is the only national, nonprofit organization that dedicates its charitable purpose to assisting communities that wish to do their best in helping local students."

Perhaps you already have a successful scholarship program in your community. Thank God that you do, but why not, at no cost to speak of, be willing to share your proven ideas with other communities so they can also be successful. This country can never be great if only your students are successful and educated. Every single student in this country should have a chance for an education to develop his or her God-given abilities to the utmost.

A Dollars for Scholars chapter also serves as an umbrella to existing independent scholarship programs that might include scholarships from service clubs, sororities, foundations, and businesses. One advantage of such an umbrella is that it allows the sponsoring organization to receive recognition for its charitable contribution while removing its burden of administration. The advantage for the student is that a single application process can cover all existing scholarship programs locally.

I know that CSFA has had the experience of coordinating up to 36 different scholarship programs in one community. The student fills out just one application, but none of the groups loses its identity. Each group's criteria are met, but more students apply and more individuals are recognized. By making the application process more efficient, each student's needs are met, and the scholarship awards are made to the most deserving young persons.

There are many other reasons why a national organization of scholarship program volunteers is a necessity for this country. For example, CSFA has emerged as a strong voice for private sector scholarship programs. The Foundation is pursuing issues with college officials and others that are crucial to making certain scholarship awards to students are utilized by colleges in the best interest of students.

Over and over, I've seen the Dollars for Scholars program work in as many different ways as there are communities in this country.

The **Wakefield, Massachusetts** chapter was started with great local leadership. One day three Bills came into my office because they heard about the success we had in Fall River. Thirty years ago, Bill Lee, Bill Spaulding, and Bill Jones sat down with me, and took all of the materials we had back to their community. They had the support of the superintendent and the media, two of the key elements to success in any community.

Now, 30 years later, the Wakefield chapter has $3 million in trust funds. From eight students helped in 1960, the number has grown to 259 in 1992. Since its inception, more than 2,600 students have been helped. There is not an individual that I know of in Wakefield who is denied an education primarily because of money. The chapter helps graduating high school seniors, college students, and adult students. If you've lost a job, you can apply for money to go back to school. If you are on welfare, you are able to apply to seek an education to get yourself in the work force.

In **Atlanta, Georgia**, public housing authorities joined forces with business, education, religious, and cultural sectors to create the city's first Dollars for Scholars chapter. With a $2,500 grant from the Allstate Foundation helping to cover the start-up costs, public housing residents themselves gave leadership to raising $50,000 in the chapter's initial year. In its first three years, more than 30 students from public housing developments have been awarded scholarships. "We started with our residents in public housing and got them involved by encouraging them to contribute one dollar to the scholarship fund," says Bettye Davis, former chapter president and executive director of the Housing Authority of Fulton County. "We want to manage this program so that parents will get involved in their children's education."

The **North Fayette, Iowa** chapter was formed by local residents during the 1989-90 Christmas break. Two years later scholarship distributions reached $28,000 for local students. "Dollars for Scholars gave us the training and administrative support to start our own community scholarship foundation," says James Boelman, president of the chapter. "The community has responded enthusiastically. We now have more than 250 donors that include individuals, businesses, and organizations. We've received generous bequests and memorial gifts, including the proceeds from a $500,000 endowment fund."

The story is repeated in towns and cities across the nation.

In **San Diego County**, the juvenile court joined with the county education office and the community to raise more than $82,000 for "at risk" students. Funds raised by the San Diego Court Schools Dollars for Scholars chapter have helped to motivate more than 130 students through scholarship awards. "For these scholarship students, the personal recognition from the community is just as important as the financial gift," says Katie O. Whalen-

Elsbree, teacher and mentor to court school DFS students. "Dollars for Scholars awards help motivate our students to stay in school. We know many of our recipients would not be in college without them."

Chapters often bring the community together. In the communities of Norway and Paris, Maine, the **Oxford Hills Dollars for Scholars** pulled together the efforts of the Kiwanis, Lions, and Rotary Clubs to create a combined endowment of over $100,000.

A partnership of the Scituate Substance Abuse Task Force and the **CSF of Scituate, Rhode Island** resulted in an annual event called "The Student Lock Up." Students who raise a minimum of $30 in pledges get to attend what amounts to a giant slumber party with free movies, games, and food.

The **Vershire Scholarship Endowment** in Vermont started a harvest festival which not only raises funds for scholarships but also supports local crafts people. The fall festival features home grown apples, wheat thrashed by hand, glass blowing, an organic pig roast, and concludes with a Civil War battle reenactment.

Bertha-Hewitt, Minnesota appealed to the community for different items or gifts to be used in a tele-auction. One home-bound woman, who lived on a fixed income, wanted to show her support but didn't have the money to contribute. She spent months preparing a beautiful quilt which not only brought in a good sum of money but also showed the young people the care and concern of the community.

Fall River, Massachusetts, the founding chapter, has already helped over 2,000 students. James Rogers has served as the president for longer than any other person in the chapter's history.

Burlington, Maine has developed an "Adopt-A-Class" program. The Lahey Clinic, a large biomedical research facility, and the local cable television company have adopted high school classes and will help with fund raising, career counseling and other activities.

Parkers Prairie, Minnesota is the home of the P-547 Club. The group, named for the school district number, was started by Lloyd Paulsen who conceived of a permanent fund developed by community members and alumni who pledged $547 or more over a four year period. To date the Club has generated over $300,000, and it recognizes people who contribute with a plaque in the high school auditorium and a newsletter which lists contributors and highlights fund-raising activities. Last year the chapter gave out scholarships to every graduating senior!

As new chapters are formed, each group continues to bring to CSFA its own unique personality and approach to the scholarship family. In their own way, each contributes to the history of the program. Sometimes they make history in their own right. The 100th Dollars for Scholars chapter was established in Indiana in 1992. The designation of chapter 100 went to the Hoosier Minority Chamber of Commerce -- Charles H. DeBow, Jr. Memorial Fund, which is an unusual, state-wide chapter based in Indianapolis.

Wherever and however CSFA chapters are formed, the program changes the lives of students and residents dramatically. The program impacts the lives of both traditional and non-traditional students. A scholarship recipient recently wrote:

"As a single parent with limited financial support I was very grateful for the scholarship I received from CSF. It was very important for me to finish my education in order to support myself and my family."

Another tells how after being dismissed from a position as Accounting Office Manager, he realized how a lack of a college education put him at a disadvantage. He wrote:

"I had many years of experience but only one year of formal education beyond high school. One of my sons was in college and the other was a year away.

"I looked for a job, but competition from better educated people made a search difficult. My wife and I determined that in order for me to be successful, I would have to return to school and complete my education.

"In January of 1982, I returned to college at the grand old age of 41 with the help of a CSF scholarship. The salary from the job my wife had and our savings were all we had to live on.

"During the three years I attended the University of Massachusetts - Boston, both of my sons were college students. At times we wondered if we would make it and if it was worth it to continue. If not for the generosity of CSF, I question if we could have made it. All three of us were recipients of very generous awards!

"Since completing my education in May of 1984 with a degree in Financial Management, I have had four jobs. In each position I have had more responsibility and earned more money..."

In Massachusetts, a women tells of how her child's learning disability made her realize that there was a need for special education teachers.

"Once my youngest child entered school, I decided to take some courses to see what life held in store for our special son. I fell in love with the idea of furthering my education and becoming a severe special needs teacher. The field was wide open...

"Once I started checking, I discovered organizations like the CSF were willing to give financial assistance to older students returning to school. Without your help, I could not have met the high tuition at Boston University," she wrote. "The CSF can take pride in assisting me in becoming a very productive teacher in our town."

Not just the recipients, but the whole community is affected by the awarding of scholarships. Norman R. Miller, superintendent of schools for Luverne, Minnesota, spoke for the country's principals and superintendents when he noted:

"The Dollars for Scholars Program has provided wonderful opportunities for a number of Luverne graduates to attend college. I am sure that in the future, Dollars for Scholars will continue to grow and hopefully provide unlimited opportunities for our young graduates to go on to school and receive training so that they will be able to compete on an international basis."

Local newspapers and other media have also reflected community response in their editorials and columns of support. The Wisconsin *Pierce County Herald* suggested:

"There are few of us who don't have the desire to live like a philanthropist...

"For most, these lifestyles of the filthy rich represent nothing more than an elusive dream. Few will hit it big at the gambling tables in Las Vegas or strike gold in some deserted mine. Yet, there's at least one way everyone can get a momentary taste of what it feels like to have a fortune, a method revealed at Ellsworth Senior High last Thursday evening.

"Dollars for Scholars not only allows the public to indulge in a practice once reserved for large corporations or the handlers of huge estates, but benefits the future leadership of our society as well. It's based on the premise that college scholarships can be funded with simple generosity from the masses instead of overwhelming bequests to local districts...

"Who knows? Such a small investment might even make participants feel like that mysteriously popular 1950's television star, 'The Millionaire.'"

Tom Grapes echoed the feelings of accomplishment in his column published by *The Union* of West Union, Iowa when he wrote:

"I just attended a NEIA Dollars for Scholars meeting and to use a Hans and Frans expression, 'I'm pumped up!' This Dollars for Scholars phenomenon is just a darn good, dynamite program. I personally feel it is one of the best ways to do something for our country. Investing in our youth is a prudent and good thing to do because the future of our country rests upon their abilities.

"In reflecting on last year's awards program, I can't help but recall the warm and gratifying feeling I had in seeing all seniors who were going on to post- high school training and/or education get an award. I think it is a majestic gesture on the part of the community to give the local grads a nice send off and well wish..."

Letters from recipients and kind words from supporters make it clear to me that, despite the statistics which paint a depressing picture of America, programs like Dollars for Scholars offer hope for our future and a glimpse of a better world for our children and grandchildren. As free people, our hands are not tied. We can still improve this country by working together, and for many, the best way to put our beliefs into action is by volunteering to help a local Dollars for Scholars chapter or by contributing to Citizens' Scholarship Foundation of America. After more than 30 years of involvement in the program, both on the local and national levels, I can't think of a better way to repay some of what this country has given to me and my family.

A complete list of Dollars for Scholars chapters, as of Spring, 1993 is found in the Appendix. Watch this list grow to over 1,000 in the near future!

Working With Colleges

The uniqueness and idealism of CSFA is that it exists to encourage our future leaders to stay in high school and to go on to higher education. It exists to give hope, opportunity, and money so they can be fed into the higher education system.

We are one of the best friends and supporters of higher educational institutions. Some of the colleges have stated that CSFA-related scholarship support is like an added endowment because of the increasing number of students coming to their campuses with scholarship money. It has been estimated that the $200,000 in CSFA scholarship aid which went to one college was the equivalent of a $3.5 million trust fund or endowment.

In 1992, over 27,000 CSFA-related scholarship recipients were attending over 2,300 different colleges and universities. For some of these institutions CSFA is beginning to make a real impact on their campuses, with over 200 students arriving with CSFA-related scholarships in hand.

Currently approximately 250 colleges and universities have joined CSFA's Collegiate Partners Program. They do so primarily because they see the benefits of CSFA's work with communities, companies, and individuals, and they want to see the organization's impact continue to grow. The appendix contains a list of CSFA's Collegiate Partners. Watch this list grow eventually to 1,000 and beyond!

Helping Business

Corporations know that unless they have trained people to hire, they cannot expand or grow. An estimated 70 percent of the work force needs training beyond a high school education. Businesses spend many billions of dollars to re-train or to train people for their particular industry, so they have a big stake in awarding money for scholarships through CSFA.

The variety of scholarship opportunities provided by CSFA for industry are as diverse as the companies that participate in the program. Some of the industries designate their scholarships for minorities, others for children of their employees, and still others for re-training, or for good will in their own area.

There are companies that provide scholarships to retrain separated employees, and a number of "fast-food" corporations provide scholarships as a way to retain their workers and to inspire them to pursue college degrees.

In fact, CSFA has custom-designed programs to fit the many varied needs of corporations, be it to help award one scholarship or 1,000.

By 1993 the list of companies, associations, and foundations using CSFA's Student Aid Management Services had grown to over 450. A list of these CSFA clients is found in the Appendix. Watch this list continue to grow rapidly as well in the years ahead!

Return on Investment

A revolutionary new concept was instituted when CSFA President Bill Nelsen gave an inspiring and clear explanation of our grass-roots organization to Representative Ken Jacobsen, chairman of the House Higher Education

Committee in the State of Washington. Jacobsen introduced legislation appropriating $100,000 to challenge towns and cities in his state to develop their own community scholarship programs. Those programs based on the CSFA Dollars for Scholars concept would receive matching funds from the state program. In one year's time, 14 new Dollars for Scholars chapters resulted from this pilot state challenge program.

This incentive grant program is a beautiful marriage of private and public initiatives in true democratic fashion. It is a perfect way to leverage any state's scholarship money. The state of Oregon has appropriated $50,000 on the same basis, and the state of Massachusetts has introduced similar legislation sponsored by Representative Edward Lambert.

A very important bill was recently introduced in the U.S. Congress. This bill would help put into place the necessary area program operations to develop Dollars for Scholars chapters in communities throughout the entire nation. Passage of this bill would result in a relatively small investment of federal funds producing millions and millions of new scholarship dollars from the private sector.

Private foundations have long known the value of CSFA and have helped education in their own states. The figures are amazing:

In Minnesota from 1976 to 1992, the original $200,000 in grants from the Bush Foundation has helped to generate $35,000,000 in corporate and community scholarships, or a ratio of 175-to-one.

In Iowa, $60,000 from the MacElroy Trust has generated $821,000 from new Dollars for Scholars chapters in two years, or a ratio of 20.5-to-one.

In Indiana, $300,000 from the Lilly Endowment has generated $2,071,000 from new Dollars for Scholars chapters in four years, or a ratio of 7-to-one.

In New York, anonymous donations of approximately $600,000 have generated $30,626,000 in corporate and community scholarships since the mid-1980's, or a ratio of 50-to-one.

Every state and region, every governmental agency and private foundation interested in helping students, needs a way to leverage their scholarship money -- and CSFA is that way!

Senator Ted Kennedy, guest speaker at 10th Anniversary of CSF of Fall River (1968). Left to right: Dr. Fradkin, Ed Berube, Senator Kennedy, Peter Friar and Joe Hanify.

Lt. Governor Elliot Richardson of Massachusetts pledges support to CSFA Board Member Ralph Seifert and Dr. Fradkin (1965).

Congratulations from Governor Michael Dukakis, with Jim Rogers, CSF of Fall River President, Barbara Kuzdzol, CSF of Massachusetts President, State Senator Mary Fonseca, and Dr. Fradkin (1977).

Senator Edward Kennedy, guest speaker at 20th Anniversary of CSF of Fall River, with State Senator Mary Fonseca, Barbara Kuzdzol, Jim Rogers, Dr. Fradkin, Representative Margaret Heckler, and Mayor Wilfred Driscoll (1978).

CSFA's national headquarters in St. Peter, Minnesota, completed in late 1984.

Vice Presidents Stu Johnson, Marlys Johnson, and President Joe Phelan at CSFA's new national headquarters (1985).

CSFA President Dr. William Nelsen receives "Sagamore of the Wabash" Award from Lt. Governor John Mutz as CSFA launches its Indiana Dollars for Scholars initiative (1987).

Dollars for Scholars volunteers Charles and Marlene Rickett congratulate Irv Fradkin and Charlotte on receiving Indiana's "Sagamore of the Wabash" award (1987).

Governor Rudy Perpich of Minnesota with Dr. Fradkin and President Nelsen at CSFA meeting in Minneapolis (1988).

James Jackson, Sister Kathleen Harrington, and Angelina Snell at the Martin Luther King, Jr. Celebration and Remembrance Day of the Interfaith Council of Greater Fall River (1988).

Patrice, Kristen, Marie, and Kathy Buonopane (left to right) are sisters and recipients of scholarship awards from CSF of Wakefield, MA.

Angela Swint, Atlanta Dollars for Scholars award recipient, with her four children. Angela is now in college on her way to realizing her dream of becoming a teacher.

Gary and Karen Halva (back) established the first endowed scholarship fund of the North Fayette (Iowa) Dollars for Scholars Foundation in memory of their son. Also pictured are their daughter Jessica and scholarship recipient Amy Palas (1992).

Shelly Goins, Yvette Crispell, Marcqk Anderson, Randi Robinson, and Katie Whalen-Elsbree of the San Diego County Court Schools Dollars for Scholars chapter (1992). Yvette and Randi are attending college with the help of Dollars for Scholars scholarships.

"All who have meditated on the art of governing man-
kind have been convinced that the fate of empires
depends on the
education of youth."

- *Aristotle*

CHAPTER 9
THE IMPORTANCE OF YOUTH INVOLVEMENT

Today, my dream is unchanged. We must provide financial aid opportunities for those students whose resources are inadequate to meet the costs of higher education. More importantly, we must make it clear that these young people have an obligation to give something back -- to repay their scholarships, when and if they can at no interest, or to volunteer their time and talents to helping the next generation of students. We must include young people in every aspect of developing our local Dollars for Scholars chapters.

It has become obvious to me, over the years, that the youth are the heart and soul of the movement. If they are invited to join in as board or committee members or as project volunteers, they give 110 percent of themselves.

The interest of the entire community and the national media indicate that Citizens' Scholarship Foundation of America is much more than a scholarship program. It has the importance, the ability and the quality of purpose to unite a community that is built upon helping and working together with our future leaders.

I have seen attitudes change when the youth join with adults in chapter activities. Not only do young people gain an appreciation for the dedicated individuals in the community who are helping them, but the adults also learn that there are some great young people in the world as well.

I have always found that a chapter became enriched and more successful when the youth participated equally with the adult leaders in planning programs and raising funds.

People often tell me, to my great satisfaction, that they feel much better about giving financial support to a chapter when they see young people looking for a hand-up, rather than a hand-out. Contributors sense this when they see young people participating in chapter activities.

Some chapters in the past formed a Youth Branch, made up of high school students with elected officers like in any club. The officers sat on the adult board of directors of the local chapter, and representatives sometimes served on chapter committees.

When the first Youth Branch was started in Fall River, it was probably the first time that parochial and public school students worked together on a project. They worked so beautifully. It was a marvelous relationship.

Every chapter should be encouraged to involve student volunteers, and perhaps a financial incentive should be given to encourage the chapters to do so. There are many by-products of getting the youth involved. They can provide peer pressure to encourage marginal students to stay in school. They gain the dignity of participating equally with adults and becoming partners in helping others.

In this way, they can see that success is not determined only by money. Success should be measured by earning a better living and doing something good for themselves. At the same time, they have to understand that in a democracy, they have to give something back.

Although it has not been proven, I believe youth involvement in CSFA chapters can help fight drug use. If peer pressure is a factor in how young people act, by working together in a good, wholesome program like CSFA, youth can see the value of education and encourage others to stay in school and to not use drugs.

We have to make youth understand that they are lucky to live in this country. They have to see that through the generosity of all different nationalities and ethnic groups, they have been given a chance for an education.

The youth are the future. But if they wish to have a future for themselves and their children, they have got to understand that they have a responsibility to help others as they have been helped.

This is nothing new. All through the ages, youth have been the future and the lifeblood of the country. Yet people complain that young people are only interested in money and self-indulgence.

I ask, why should they be surprised when so much of the media displays and advertises all of the negative side of our country -- violence, murder, greed, and the like. Where are the programs and media that demonstrate what is good about America? There are many examples of people who came up the hard way, who live the American dream. People should be shown their good deeds and examples to better themselves, their neighbors and their communities.

If you want to develop our most precious assets -- the minds of the young people -- then you who control the advertising, television and other media must tell the positive side and must give America back to the Americans.

Most importantly, however, we, the founder and officers, the chapter leaders and scholarship recipients, must set an example for our young people. We have to show them that democracy is alive and well and that America can be made even better if we all work toward that goal. If we do that, then I will know that all the traveling and sacrifice will have been worth it and my dream will come true.

CHAPTER 10
ATTRACTING GREAT PEOPLE TO THE CAUSE

CSFA has succeeded primarily because it has attracted dedicated people, staff and volunteers, to its cause. To mention all the great people who have helped to shape and grow the organization is not possible in this type of book, but I must point to those key groups of individuals who have been formally recognized already for their lasting contributions.

The Honor Roll Trustees is a relatively new group, but it is made up of wonderful people who have over 200 years of combined experience serving CSFA. All of them have made a great contribution to Citizens' Scholarship Foundation of America, having served CSFA as president, officer, or a valued member of the Board of Directors.

The Honor Roll Trustees group began under the leadership of CSFA Board member Frank Morin. He recognized that key Trustees, even after their official service was over still felt that CSFA was of such value to America, and that they had such a good time and enjoyed such rapport with each other, they would like to continue to serve in some capacity. He and several other Board members began to ask: "How can we do something to keep outstanding Trustees involved?"

The Honor Roll Trustee organization was formed primarily to advise and counsel CSFA's president in whatever way he saw fit. The Honor Roll Trustees do not make policy or to tell the president what to do, but serve at his discretion.

As far as we know, this is the first time in history that such an organization has been formed. When asked, the Honor Roll Trustees share with the president and the

Board information, ideas, and expertise to help continue the growth of the organization.

To become a member, a person must serve CSFA as a Board member for at least six years, and two years must elapse after that service before being elected by the Board of Trustees to the Honor Roll.

As a group, we meet three times a year, and one individual serves as chair on a rotating basis. It is great to get together not just to offer suggestions and ideas, but to renew old friendships.

What has always impressed me about CSFA is the quality of the people who get involved. The Honor Roll Trustees are a perfect example of the wonderful people who are helping make the dream of democracy come alive in America today.

Members of the Honor Roll Trustees, as of May 1992, are:

Dr. Irving Fradkin - CSFA Founder

Joseph M. Hinchey - Former Senior Vice President, Analog Devices, Dollars for Scholars volunteer, and outstanding Board member for nine years.

Barbara M. Kuzdzol - Director of Development, Worchester Children's Friend Society, Dollars for Scholars recipient and chapter volunteer, dedicated Board member for more than a decade.

Edward M. Lee - Attorney, Westfield, Massachusetts, former Chair of the Board, dedicated volunteer and fundraiser.

Greg J. Macri, Jr. - President, GJ Products, chapter volunteer and dedicated Board member for nine years.

Howard A. Moreen - Business consultant, former director of contributions for Aetna Life, outstanding Board member. (We mourned the passing of Howard during the time this book was being prepared.)

Frank E. Morin - President, Affiliated Consulting Services, Inc., national leader among school counselors; as Board member he gave leadership to shaping the organization.

William B. Norris - Attorney from Cleveland, Ohio, former Board chair.

Joseph F. Phelan - President, University of New Hampshire Foundation, served with great commitment and skill as CSFA's Executive Director and President.

Ralph H. Seifert - Former President of New England Security, chapter volunteer and president, former Board Chair, currently Chair of CSFA's National Campaign.

David Logan Steele - Vice President, Trusts, Merchants Bank, Pennsylvania, former Treasurer of the Board and long-time Board member.

Eugene C. Struckhoff - Former President of Council on Foundations and Baltimore Community Foundation, first Chair of the CSFA Board.

Recently CSFA has begun recognizing other persons who have played key roles in building the organization while serving somewhat shorter periods of time on the

Governing Board. Among these outstanding people named as CSFA Trustees Emeriti are Tom Bellinger of New York, Harold Hebl of Minnesota, Don James of Massachusetts, Harry Rosenberg, of Florida, and Ed Shapiro of New Hampshire. But chief among this group is Leslie S. Hubbard, former Chairman of the Board of Hubbard Farms in Walpole, New Hampshire. Les, now in his nineties, cares deeply about the future of young people and has many times helped CSFA through his generous gifts to expand its work. And he has assured that the work of CSFA in service to its Dollars for Scholars in the New England area will continue because of his gift to endow the New England office through his estate. Les exemplifies the best of the American ideal of people helping people.

Recently the CSFA Board, through the leadership of former President Joe Phelan, initiated the Milestone Award for people who have made real differences at crucial times in the life of the organization. Recipients to date have included: David McLaughlin, President of the Toro Company in 1976 when that company became CSFA's first corporate client; John Lynn, Executive Director of the Lilly Endowment in Indiana in the 1970's when CSFA first expanded its Dollars for Scholars work to the Midwest; Jean Hennessey, past president of the New Hampshire Charitable Fund during the 1970's, when CSFA began helping to manage scholarship programs beyond its Dollars for Scholars community level; and the late Gove Sleeper, Massachusetts businessman who made the first major deferred gift to the organization, a gift that is now part of CSFA's endowment and helps the organization every year to impact the lives of more students.

I am personally grateful to all the people who have been attracted to CSFA's unique and far-reaching mission. My life has been blessed by them and so have the students who have been the ultimate beneficiaries of their service.

CHAPTER 11
THE IMPACT ON PEOPLE

Have the people associated with Citizens' Scholarship Foundation of America made a difference in the lives of others? We can answer with a resounding, Yes! The record tells us so. We can point to the many successes of people touched by CSFA programs. And we can tell very well by the personal testimonies of former scholarship recipients.

Successes of Scholarship Recipients

Over the years, there have been many, many success stories in CSFA. Here is a look at some of them.

William Reilly grew up in Fall River, Massachusetts, where smokestacks from the textile mills once sent pollutants into the environment. As Director of the Environmental Protection Agency, he made sure that industries would comply with the Clean Air Bill, which he helped to craft in 1990.

Reilly received one of the first CSF scholarships in 1958. He graduated from Yale University, received a law degree from Harvard University, and earned a masters' degree from Columbia University.

Currently, he lives in Alexandria, Virginia, and in addition to continuing to work for environmental organizations, he serves on numerous public and private boards. Like many others, his lessons in democracy learned from the examples set by those in his CSF chapter weren't forgotten.

Les Kretman was one of the many young people who got involved with Citizens' Scholarship Foundation when it began in Fall River, Massachusetts. As a member of the

Youth Branch, he helped organize fund-raisers for the new organization. By contributing time and energy, he helped shape CSF of Fall River into the successful organization it is today.

Kretman has also done well. He received a CSF scholarship in 1960 which helped him attend Boston University where he graduated with a degree in broadcast journalism. Today, he is a producer of NBC news in Washington.

"It feels pretty good to have been a part of something so successful," he said.

Tamara Patasky never guessed her part-time job at Burger King would help fund her college education as much as it did. But her participation in the CSFA-managed Burger King Crew Educational Assistance Program helped finance her studies at Miami-Dade Community College. The college also helped provide funds as part of their participation in the CEAP Matching Funds Network.

"The CEAP scholarship helped make it possible for me to go to college," she said. "My parents thought it was great because they were not able to help me as much as they would have liked, and being the independent person that I am, this was one way I could earn the money to pay for school myself."

Patasky continued to work for Burger King while in college, then left the company to join Southeast Bank in Miami, Florida as a customer service representative, and then as assistant to the administrator of international trusts.

Gary Willis received a scholarship from the Mansfield, Massachusetts Chapter and learned a lesson in helping others. He returned to the community and became the youngest chapter president ever, an office which was later held by his wife and his mother. What an active Dollars for Scholars family!

Professionally, Willis served as president of the Foxboro Company (a Fortune 500 company) for several years and is currently president of ZYGO Corporation, a growing high-tech company headquartered in Connecticut. He remains active in CSFA by serving on the Foundation's Board of Trustees.

John Harty became president and CEO of the Pepsi Co. Building Systems in 1981, but without CSFA help, he doubts it would have been possible.

"Without scholarships, it wouldn't have been possible for me to attend Notre Dame, and my life would have developed very differently," he admitted.

Harty grew up in Fall River and was aware of the scholarship program. He received one of the first awards in 1958. Over the years, he has not forgotten the help he received. He has served on the Tulsa, Oklahoma planning commission, as well on numerous community boards including those for educational and non-profit organizations.

Mark Kaplan likes to help people, and as a pharmacist, he feels he is doing just that. He also knows that he has to thank the people of Stafford Springs, Connecticut, who helped his parents pay his expenses at the University of Connecticut.

Kaplan received one of the first scholarships from the Stafford Springs CSF in 1963. After graduating from the University of Connecticut, he worked in several hospitals as Director of Pharmacy, was chosen Massachusetts Hospital Pharmacist of the Year in 1984, and served as president of the New England Council of Hospital Pharmacists. But he hasn't forgotten how it all started.

"I have always been honored to have been in the first group of scholarship recipients," he said. "I hope to be able to continue to repay this award in the future to help ensure that other Stafford graduates will be able to receive scholarships."

Anne Stalley graduated in 1984 and planned to attend DePauw University in Indiana. Although her financial aid wasn't enough to cover her expenses, her mother worked for the Toro Company. The company came through with a four-year scholarship, managed by CSFA.

"The scholarship from Toro showed me that other people thought that my education was as important as I did," she said, adding that it was her education and volunteer community experiences that made her want to pursue a career in social work.

Stalley not only graduated from DePauw, she went on to receive a graduate degree in social service administration from the University of Chicago. Over the years, she has helped others as she had been helped, by working as a peer counselor, a Big Sister, and helping the needy in Guatemala.

Joseph Macy probably would still have attended Brown University in Providence, Rhode Island without the help of the scholarship he received from CSF of Fall River, Massachusetts in 1961, but more valuable than the money was the lesson in democracy that he learned.

"More important to me then, and now, was the Citizens' Scholarship Foundation as an expression of community confidence in its young people and the fact that the scholarship funds were generated from a broad-based community appeal as opposed to a single donor or foundation," he said, "This expression of community spirit and support was very important to me while I was at Brown."

After he graduated, he established a law practice in Fall River and became active in the Citizens' Scholarship Foundation. Macy established two memorial scholarships, one in his uncle's name and the other in his father's name.

"I feel this is the very least a former recipient can do, and I only wish that more people who have benefitted from Citizens' Scholarships contributed to the local fund," he said.

When **Patricia Eagan** graduated in 1969 from B.M.C. Durfee High School in Fall River, Massachusetts, Citizens' Scholarship Foundation helped pay for her education at Framingham State College. In 1991, she decided it was time to help pay them back.

As the philatelic clerk at the Fall River Post Office, she sold her share of stamps and became involved in a number of special cancellations. She thought a special cancellation to mark the 15th anniversary of the CSF Christmas Arts and Crafts Fair would be appropriate. It was not only a great idea -- it helped raise about $1,000 for the local scholarship fund.

"It's great," she suggested. "I feel like I'm giving something back."

Returning the Favor

Over the years, I have met many marvelous people who have contributed a great deal to help CSFA grow. Some, like Barbara Kuzdzol, have been helped by a scholarship, but then came back and assisted many, many others.

Barbara received a scholarship in Mansfield, Massachusetts and went on to become a teacher. As an educator, she continued to work with CSF, serving as president of CSF of Massachusetts and as a member of the national Board of Trustees. Other New England volunteers like Ralph Seifert helped many communities establish chapters, as did Kevin Lally and Patricia Mooney in Wakefield, Mass.

One of the more unusual stories is that of Bob Alin. After retiring from business, he went on to become a Dollars for Scholars volunteer director in North Dakota, after business owner Fred Scheel donated $100,000 to stimulate chapters by offering challenge grants of $2,000. Alin traveled across the state and by December of 1992, 37 chapters were established, with a goal of 50 by the end of 1993.

In addition to repaying CSFA by helping spread the program in their communities and surrounding areas, many scholarship recipients are asked to accept the moral obligation to repay their awards when and if possible. Many have done that, and others have gone on to establish their own scholarships.

The following are excerpts from some of the thousands of thank you letters which have been received over the years. They provide a glimpse into some of the people who have been helped -- and who will in turn help others.

"The Citizens' Scholarship Foundation made it possible for me to attend the Union Hospital School of Nursing from 1963-1966, and we are hoping this money will aid another student's endeavors.

"It is a $100 scholarship in memory of Evelyn H. Cooper for a student contemplating studies at the Fall River

Diploma School of Nursing given by Mr. and Mrs. Andre A. Langlais."

- Russlyn Cooper Langlais

"Just a few lines expressing my appreciation for the scholarship awarded to me. I am proud to have been awarded the scholarship in memory of your mother and father, and I hope I am worthy of it."

- Everett Aguiar, Jr.

"I've been meaning to write to you and offer my contribution to the CSF for quite some while now, but with school and exams at Bridgewater, I've had my hands full.

"I'm afraid my contribution doesn't come close to the award that I received last year, but I am aware that every little bit counts, having stood in the street last year, adding up those nickels, dimes and quarters, ending up with quite a sum...

"Enclosed is a $10 contribution from my sister Pauline, who received her award in '67 - '68

- a $5 contribution from my brother Daniel, who was given his certificate of award from CSF for '68 - '69

- and my $5 contribution. (I received my award for the year 1971 - 1972.)"

- Muriel Dumas

"CSF gave me a chance. I want to repay that chance. Even though I'm not obligated, once I'm financially better off I intend on giving some money to CSF. I want to be able to help someone get the education I got."

- Debbie Hodge

"Anderson Little Company and Employees:

"I deeply appreciate and am very grateful that your company could help me further my education by donating some money to the Citizens' Scholarship Foundation of Fall River. By your giving them a scholarship, you helped them give me a scholarship and many other boys and girls who want to continue their education.

"I feel that if there were more companies and businesses around like you to help when help is needed by the scholarship foundation, then many more teens could go to college. Please keep up your kindness and good will and help scholarship foundations as much as possible. Maybe if there were more companies who are willing to give up some money to help more teens get to college, then maybe there wouldn't be many hippies hanging around Fall River."

- John Joseph Fortin

"Thank you so very much for giving me the step to beginning my journey of 1,000 miles into nursing. I hope some day I may be able to help some other student help herself into nursing. It meant so much to know so many people really cared!"

- Jeanne L. Cadrin

"Enclosed please find a bank check for $25 for this year's drive to the Foundation. Please accept this as sort of a thank you for your efforts during all these years in aiding deserving students. You and the foundation helped my daughter Ann Marie last year.

"I recall last year's award exercise and found the experience most rewarding. You people created a deep, warm feeling of helping others. All those involved in your committee seem down to earth, humble, dedicated people. All I can say is it felt good just to be present."

- Mr. and Mrs. Walter Plaziak

"I want to thank you for having established an organization such as the 'Dollars for Scholars.' In my haste at the awards presentation, I fear I did not thank you properly. I had already acknowledged the individual sponsors, but I feel that you should receive the greatest thanks since, without you, none of it would be possible.

"The receipt of my scholarship has enabled my to meet my expenses at Providence College. Without it, I would have placed a greater burden on my family. I hope I may be of service to the committee in the future and would be most willing to aid at fund raising functions...."

- Judith A. Medeiros

"You have urged us many times not to forget our benefactors, but all members of CSF deserve at least as much of this gratitude for their unselfish donations of their own lives and time.

"I am working very hard to deserve this help and am succeeding somewhat, as I did make the dean's list last semester. I do hope to continue the good work.

"Thank you again and I do hope that you can continue this excellent program, and that some day I can contribute also."

- Nanette Lavoie

"...The reason for this letter is to tell you how much I appreciate your help. Without this assistance, I would never have been able to keep up with the ever growing list of books and supplies needed for these courses. I hope in the future I will be able to make this same assistance possible for someone else...."

- Denise Roussel

"I would like to take this opportunity to thank the Citizens' Scholarship Foundation for the generous scholarship I have received.

"If at any time in the future I can be of service to the Foundation, I will be more than happy to do so."

- Jean K. Souza

"I just thought I would write to tell you that my first semester at Framingham State College was fantastic! The numerous friends met and experiences encountered were irreplaceable...

"At this time, I feel extremely grateful to the many people who have helped me toward attaining my goal. I truly hope that many others will be assisted in the years to come."

- Carole J. Arruda

"Let's face it. If it wasn't for the scholarships, we never would have been able to afford coming here. The cost of books alone is staggering."

- Barbara Simcock

"Since I am a former recipient of a scholarship, I am always more than happy to answer your appeal each year. I hope that my financial status will allow me to increase my donation each year, as I am doing so this year.

"Please convey my thanks to your organization for the generous help they have given to me and my sister (Rose A. Ciarpella, B.M.C. Durfee High School Class of '65). Without the aid given to my family during those six years we were at college, our education would have been very difficult to attain.

"You might be interested to know that Rose is with the Peace Corps, teaching mathematics in Botswana, Africa. I am completing my fifth year of instruction with the department of mathematics at Tiverton Jr.- Sr. High School. These positions, which we both enjoy, were in part made possible by the labors of your organization.

"Therefore, accept this check in partial payment of my 'debt' to your organization and my best wishes with your current projects."

- Edward S. Ciarpella

"I've been on welfare and because I was able to come back to school, I was able to get off the welfare rolls. This is the best thing to happen to me. I couldn't have done it without the scholarships."

- Denise Duclos

"The scholarship I received from the Citizens' Scholarship Foundation of Fall River enabled me to complete four years of study at Wheaton College in Illinois. Without help from the citizens of Fall River who demonstrated vision and commitment to liberal arts education through establishing the scholarship program, I doubt that I would have been able to fulfill my dream of receiving a college degree.

"Of course, my experience in college was so positive that it led me to further study and preparation for service and leadership in higher education, both at a major university and later at a small liberal arts college.

"In 1958 there were very few programs available to provide financial assistance for those of us from financially-limited backgrounds. The Citizens' Scholarship

Foundation of Fall River was conceived at the right moment in my personal life. Your foresight and leadership made a lasting impact on me. Little did I know upon receiving this scholarship that this experience would shape my mission in life so dramatically.

"I've enclosed an article of Gordon College's *Stillpoint* magazine which announced my appointment as president in the summer of 1992. Thank you for your encouragement over 30 years ago."

-R. Judson Carlberg, President
Gordon College (Mass.)

Literally thousands of similar responses have come to me and to CSFA's leaders and volunteers throughout the country. They demonstrate that what we are doing is highly worthwhile. They show that each one of us can make a positive difference in the lives of others. They inspire me to keep going. They should inspire more and more Americans to help others with the help of Citizens' Scholarship Foundation of America.

Dr. Fradkin becomes the first person to receive the key to Fall River from two different mayors (1989).

CSFA Governing Board at Burger King national headquarters in Florida (1989).

Marie Willis of Mansfield, Massachusetts receives Dollars for Scholars National Honor Roll Award from Dr. Fradkin, with Barbara Kuzdzol, Gary Willis (her son and CSFA Board member), and Joe Hinchey looking on (1989).

Chamber President Mark Montigny and Superintendent of Schools John Correiro of Fall River congratulate Dr. Fradkin on his receiving the "Giraffe Award," a national award for those who "stick their necks out" to help others (1989).

New Hampshire businessman Les Hubbard (middle) receives CSFA Trustee Emeritus award from Dr. Fradkin, Greg Macri, Hayden Smith, and President Bill Nelsen (1991).

CSFA Trustees Honor Roll members gather at meeting in Walpole, New Hampshire (1992).

Board members Hayden Smith and John Wedum with President Bill Nelsen and Executive Vice President Marlys Johnson at meeting in San Antonio, Texas (1992).

Metropolitan Boys Choir sings tribute to Dr. Fradkin at campaign kick-off in Minneapolis, Minnesota

Milestone Award winner David McLaughlin, president of the Aspen Institute, with Lloyd Brandt, CSFA Board Chair, Dr. Fradkin, and Joe Hinchey, Honor Roll Trustees member (1992).

Kathleen Kennedy Townsend (third from left) serves as keynote speaker for 35th Anniversary Banquet of the CSF of Fall River (April, 1993). Others pictured: Steve Pratt, New England Dollars for Scholars Area Director, Rev. Robert Lawrence, Dr. Fradkin, President Nelsen, Rabbi William Kaufman, Jim Rogers, CSF of Fall River president, and Les Kretman, NBC News producer and member of CSFA's National Advisory Board.

CSFA Executive Team -- Stuart Johnson, Bill Nelsen, Steve Cramer, Marlys Johnson, Marilyn Rundell, and Fred Vogel on business planning retreat (1993).

Dr. Fradkin continues to speak for the cause of building a better America through education.

"Worse than being blind would be
to be able to see but not have any wisdom."
—Helen Keller

CHAPTER 12
SCHOLARSHOP

by David Bach, Vice President for Community Programs,
Citizens' Scholarship Foundation of America

For much of its history, Citizens' Scholarship Foundation of America helped youth move from high school to postsecondary education by providing scholarships. Yet CSFA's leaders, including founder Dr. Irving Fradkin, have increasingly realized that many youth who had great potential were dropping out of school or abandoning the idea of going to college during middle school or high school.

In response, CSFA developed new programs to reach students at earlier ages—programs that would challenge and assist youth to understand the value of education, stay in school, and prepare to enter and succeed in postsecondary education. Consequently, these youth would be able to compete for scholarships from Dollars for Scholars chapters, from sponsors of scholarship programs administered by Scholarship Management Services, and from other scholarship opportunities.

Some Dollars for Scholars chapters had already started reaching out to youth in elementary and junior high through academic enrichment programs, mentoring, and tutoring. Several programs administered by Scholarship Management Services had provided "set-aside" scholarships for junior high or high school students who could claim the scholarship funds for college only if they stayed in school and had other specific academic and personal goals. However, a more formal and far-reaching program was needed.

In the mid-1990s, Marlys Johnson, then executive vice president for CSFA, was asked to create a new program area. She developed the name and concept of ScholarShop, a program with a curriculum and multi-media resource center designed to motivate and prepare young people to achieve their full potential as students and as productive members of society. Her goal was to implement the program and resource center in local communities in cooperation with other youth-serving organizations. Johnson obtained start-up funds, hired consultants to develop the

ScholarShop curriculum, and pre-tested the program at several sites, including the Ketchum YMCA in inner-city Los Angeles and several Boys and Girls Clubs in Fort Worth, Texas.

Following several program adjustments, Cargill, a worldwide leader in agribusiness headquartered in Minnesota, made a major grant to help establish ScholarShop in local communities where it had plant operations throughout the United States. Subsequent grants from Cargill and other national, regional, and local supporters have helped to spread the program to 172 locations throughout the nation as of July, 2002.

ScholarShop is a fresh way of approaching career and postsecondary exploration with teens. The curriculum includes learning about oneself, careers, colleges, and other postsecondary schools through seven modules designed to move students from self-understanding to preparation for life and learning. The modules are:

1. Looking Inward (self-esteem)
2. Windows of Interest (career options)
3. Windows of Opportunity (postsecondary options)
4. Windows to College (college options)
5. Looking to the Future (college admissions and financial aid)
6. Windows of Service (community service)
7. Windows of Change (transition from high school to college)

ScholarShop's curriculum was inspired by and is updated annually with the advice of teachers and youth program leaders around the country. It pulls together fresh ideas for the curriculum, gathers some of the best software, videos, books, magazines and pamphlets for the resource library, and folds them all together into a program designed to increase high school graduation rates and increase postsecondary enrollment and graduation rates.

For schools, colleges, and youth-serving agencies with existing programs for career and college exploration, ScholarShop is a tool to make the process easier. With the latest in print, video, and software resources, updated annually, staff can concentrate on what they do best, teach. It is a comprehensive curriculum that can fill in gaps in existing programs and provide alternative ways of reaching students, some of whom may be falling through the cracks. And the curriculum is flexible and can be easily integrated into social studies and career classes in schools, Black Achievers and teen leadership programs at YMCAs, and a variety of teen programs at Boys and Girls Clubs.

For organizations that do not currently have a career and college exploration program, ScholarShop pulls together all the pieces needed for a comprehensive program, including a thorough curriculum with detailed lesson plans, a resource library of books, magazines and videos, and computer software that is updated every year. Display materials are also included to create a visual presence for the program.

The curriculum also creates a place for teens to gather. ScholarShop's resource library encourages youth to gather and explore careers and colleges using entertaining multi-media computer software, and to do research together with the many books and magazines provided.
ScholarShop is different from other career and college exploration programs in that it helps youth take time to understand who they are, what they enjoy doing, and what skills and aptitudes they have to contribute. The program then steers youth to explore the many careers that are possible, what lifestyles they require and the day-to-day activities that make up those careers. Finally, the youth can decide on a career and the colleges, or other postsecondary institutions or training programs, that can help them obtain the best education to reach their goals.

While technology makes more information available to youth than ever before, processing such a mass of information requires interaction with peers and caring adults. ScholarShop emphasizes the interaction of youth and caring adults in a safe place to share who they are, and make choices about who they want to become.

ScholarShop is a network of people who share a common love and concern for the youth of today. ScholarShop training is the first opportunity for new ScholarShop coordinators to build relationships with people from around the country and share knowledge and experiences. ScholarShop conferences are held to further build this network and bring forward the latest ideas used by teachers and other youth-serving professionals. The Scholarshop Coordinator News provides tips on how other sites are using ScholarShop and quarterly information packs provide new resources for local programs gathered from around the ScholarShop network and beyond.

ScholarShops are encouraged to call or email other ScholarShops to learn more about their successes. Regular conference calls and chat rooms are coordinated by the ScholarShop national office to connect coordinators around the country.

Two new components of ScholarShop are ScholarShop Jr. and ParentShop, which were created and designed to expand the program to new audiences.

ScholarShop Jr. is a curriculum and resource library designed for elementary students in grades 4 through 6. Presented in a highly motivational, hands-on format, it explores the same issues as ScholarShop with materials appropriately developed for this age.

ParentShop is a series of interactive workshops addressing how parents can support and encourage learning, understand unique learning styles, and explore careers with their children. It also addresses how to be an effective advocate for your child in school and how to navigate the application and scholarship process for postsecondary education.

CSFA's vision for ScholarShop is to reach more and more youth in communities throughout the country, to get them excited about the value of education, and to encourage them to enter and succeed in postsecondary education. To expand ScholarShop, CSFA will continue to work with national and regional partners, such as Boys and Girls Clubs, YMCAs, churches, and Dollars for Scholars chapters. It also will place much of the valuable ScholarShop content on the Internet in various forms to reach even wider audiences. Plans have been developed for a highly animated, interactive online version of ScholarShop available at the click of a mouse that will expand access to ScholarShop to thousands of additional youth nationwide. The anticipated online launch date of ScholarShop is the fall of 2003.

The ScholarShop program truly works, and CSFA will improve and expand it to reach even more youth in the years to come.

CHAPTER 13
THE AMERICAN DREAM CHALLENGE

by Dr. Irving A. Fradkin

How exciting it has been to see the thousands of students going on to colleges, universities, and vocational schools as a result of the continually expanding work and service of Citizens' Scholarship Foundation of America. Yet, I have been deeply disturbed by the number of youth who drop out of school, get involved in drugs or crime, or become pregnant and fail to realize their potential.

In my mind, children are a garden of special treasures that we should nurture and nourish. Education is vital to their future and the future of our nation because a good education allows every child to pursue the American Dream, to rise to the next level and to make a valuable contribution to our society. But, our youth need to be inspired and motivated at early stages of their lives.

Based on these key concerns and beliefs, in 1994, I created the American Dream Challenge as an early outreach program of the Dollars for Scholars chapter in Fall River, Massachusetts.

The purpose of the American Dream Challenge is to encourage students in the fourth, sixth, eighth and tenth grades to stay in school. Later, when they are seniors in high school, Dollars for Scholars can continue to support and help them realize their higher education goals with additional scholarship support.

Through the American Dream Challenge, students receive scholarships at an early age that will encourage them to stay in school and aspire to higher education.

Beginning in fourth grade, students participate in the American Dream Challenge by pledging to stay in school, be drug and violence free, perform community service, and respect other cultures, religions, and ethnic backgrounds. Students also write an essay detailing their thoughts on the importance of education.

Essay winners are selected in the fourth, sixth, eighth and tenth grades. A committee of community and chapter leaders selects the winners. These students receive the following scholarships in the form of savings bonds that are set aside in a bank account until they begin their postsecondary education:

Since its inception in 1994, as of July 2002, the American Dream Challenge has awarded $110,200 to approximately 740 students and expanded the grade level participation from solely fourth grade to now fourth, sixth, eighth and tenth grade.

Implementing the American Dream Challenge

- In Fall River, the program committee for the American Dream Challenge is formed by enrolling past board members from Dollars for Scholars chapters and other interested citizens who wish to work with younger students.

- The full cooperation and support of the Superintendent of Schools office is vital to the success of the program.

- All information pertaining to the essays and awards is sent out to the various classes by the school.

- All essays—the top three from each classroom as submitted by the teacher—are directed to a central location. The awards committee selects the outstanding essay.

- The winner in each class is then notified through the school. Some of the teachers will have the winning essay read in their classes and posted on their bulletin boards.

- Arrangements also might be made to announce the winning essays in a public place or have the winners read them on the radio.

Suggested Timetable for the American Dream Challenge

January	First meeting of the American Dream Challenge committee will be held. Decide if the school is going to award scholarships or certificates. Set up a fund-raising committee if needed. Decide on the topic for the essay.
February	Information and topic is given to the teachers. Students write essay in class. Essays given to awards committee.

March	Awards committee selects winning essays. The winners of each class are informed through the offices of the school. Date of awards ceremony is finalized.
April	Speaker plans are set, usually at a school facility. Publicity also should include videotaping, local media, and other promotion methods.
May or June	Presentation of the awards.

Value to the Community

- The American Dream Challenge gets elementary schools involved in the college planning process at an early age and helps keep students on the path toward postsecondary education.
- Cross-sections of the community–including people of all racial and ethnic backgrounds, ages and professions–come together to become involved in a volunteer project.
- People receive gratification by donating time and money to make the future better for the next generation.
- Caring citizens seek to combat racism and prejudice by getting children and adults to know and respect each other.
- The community as a whole becomes more aware of the value of education and the importance of educators.

The Positive Effects on Children

- The essay encourages children at an early age to think about the value of education and how it will benefit them in the future. It can motivate students to stay in school and go on to higher education.
- It promotes positive values and idealism for children. By emphasizing education as a goal in life, it promotes a greater desire to become a better student.
- It can motivate all students, especially the marginal students, to improve their learning skills.

- Children are exposed to various members of the community as role models who show genuine concern and support for them to succeed.

"The hard truth is that in a free society the ultimate responsibility rests with the people themselves. It is our beliefs, our behavior, and our philosophy that have in many instances changed for the worse. Our injury is self-inflicted; the good news is that what has been self-inflicted can be self-corrected."

—William Bennett, January, 1994

CHAPTER 14
LIVING HEROES, UNSUNG HEROES, AND CHOICES: COMPONENTS OF THE AMERICAN DREAM CHALLENGE

by H.B. Ussach, Teacher, Fall River, Massachusetts

Big words from a former education secretary and the co-founder of Empower America, words of both inspiration and motivation. If you do not believe him, here are similar words from a Fall River, Massachusetts, fourth-grader several years ago. Megan Paquett's winning essay in the American Dream Challenge said in part: "Each person is responsible for reaching their own goal.... never give up." Where can persons find this determination to succeed? Who can offer inspiration, motivation, and a big dose of cheerleading? Heroes!

To fill this need in young persons' lives for heroes, Dr. Irving Fradkin felt it was necessary to keep innovating beyond the original scope of Citizens' Scholarship Foundation of America (CSFA). It is not enough to only award scholarship money toward higher education. Fradkin saw a need to excite and motivate students as early as fourth grade to finish high school, and he devised a competitive way to secure funds for some of them to use if they go on to college. He and other education experts identified fourth grade as a critical developmental year when learning and behavioral problems start to surface and future high school dropouts can be targeted for turnaround.

Perpetual scholarships, set up to memorialize a loved one or to honor a deserving individual, engage the attention and inspiration of young students. Here's how it works: A two-paragraph biography of the honoree accompanies a check for a one-time, $2,000 tax-free grant toward a permanent scholarship. The money is deposited in a local bank in the honoree's name. The interest only, in the amount of $100, will be awarded to a fourth grader when he/she graduates from high school and goes on to higher education. The fourth grader signs a pledge to do his/her best in school, drug-and-alcohol free, without resorting to violence to settle disputes.

American Dream Challenge's three components—Living Heroes, Unsung Heroes, and Choices—are another example of grassroots activism that works. Just as CSFA started locally in 1958 with a one dollar contribution, expanded rapidly to $4,500 and eventually became a national endowment organization awarding, as of July 2002, $911.5 million to nearly 850,000 deserving students, over its life, Fradkin's 1994 idea, the American Dream Challenge, also might go nationwide. It probably will, considering Fradkin's incredible energy, innovation, and willingness to continue as an unpaid volunteer to keep students in school.

The three components are self-contained and functioning, related or interchangeable, depending upon a community's needs or requirements to keep students focused on long-range goals. Why is it important?

Students from fourth grade up see 16, 17, and 18-year-olds achieving business and artistic success in computers, dot-com startups, services, music, and filmmaking, and they also want to be out there making their mark. They feel they are missing out on something. They are bored with school, unmindful of teachers and other adults and rude to each other. They are rushing pell-mell, living fast, playing fast, driving fast, talking fast, but thinking too slowly, adopting bad habits and behavior, and making poor choices. In this warp-speed society, young people can easily get distracted from their goals. Some may also end up in prison.

Living Heroes

The Living Heroes component of the American Dream Challenge offers students positive role models—people who model ethical behavior and time-tested virtues of hard work, dedication, and commitment. Almost 10 years ago, fifth and sixth graders in one school had so little understanding of heroes that they could only choose cartoon characters and professional wrestlers as models to emulate. Why? Because they placed too much value on material or superficial things like money, TV exposure, strength and good looks. A third grader in another school told his teacher he did not have to obey her because his dad made more money than he did. (Thomas Lickona, Educating for Character, 1991).

Today, the situation is still bad. During the 1999-2000 academic year, sixth, seventh, and eighth grade English students at a Fall River middle school again chose cartoon characters and professional wrestlers when asked to asked to write 300-word character profiles.

Living Heroes come from all walks of life: government, law, business, religion, medicine, education, and community service. They exhibit enduring qualities and values such as self-control, self-discipline, courage, fairness, tolerance, compassion, honesty, prudence, and competence." Schools must teach the five Rs—reading, riting, rithmetic, respect, and responsibility" (Lickona).

Living Heroes are all around us. Every town has them. Here are some from Fall River:

1. Mayor Edward Lambert, who was encouraged to graduate from college and devote his life to public service. He started on the school committee, went to the state legislature, and then the city's top office. He still visits local schools to talk to students about city history and the challenge and rewards of public service.

2. Two local state senators, Joan Menard and Tom Norton, began as teachers. Not content to stand and deliver history and information to students or see problems around them, they ran for public office.

3. Reverend Robert Lawrence of the First Congregation Church grew up as a farm boy. He labored to become ordained, worked as a prison chaplain, obtained his own pulpit and was named Person of the Year in Fall River.

4. Superintendent of Schools James Gibney grew up in very modest circumstances, working as a golf caddie and even a shoeshine boy to finish school. He was determined to become a teacher to share knowledge and learning with others. He succeeded, and his capable management skills propelled him into school administration.

Here are other Living Heroes:

5. Globe Manufacturing Company founder Thomas A. Rodgers, Jr., guided his firm for 50 years, contributed to the community

and offered scholarships and incentives to his employees' families. Rodgers was the first Fall River company president to believe in and make a sizeable contribution to Citizens' Scholarship Foundation of America.

6. Police officer Thomas J. Guinta was killed in the line of duty. The son of a police officer, Thomas often worked with at-risk youth to speak out against crime and drugs. Thomas' brother, Timothy, is a policeman too.

7. Attorney Antonio Luongo worked his way through high school and college in a diner. He joined the U.S. Army paratroopers and became a captain in the reserves. Later while attending law school, he operated a small restaurant and worked as an insurance adjuster.

These Living Heroes can inspire others:

8. Chong Gong Wong, father of Betty Chang, present owner of China Royal Restaurant, was born in China in 1911 and came to the U.S. in 1932. He worked hard during the Depression as a farmer and in a laundromat, sending most of his money back to his wife in China. Years went by until he was able to start a small restaurant and bring his wife here from China.

9. Everett Durfee Chapman died in his eighties running an outreach ministry for the elderly, which he also founded. While working as a career accountant, he also was a professional musician, church organist, and faithful participant in church services and activities.

10. Michael Konarski struggled all his life with muscular dystrophy. He attended public school each day on crutches, endured many hospital stays, and when he could no longer physically go to school in seventh grade, he received classroom instruction via an intercom system. Konarski managed to graduate from Durfee High School in this way. He was an avid reader all his life of World War II military history, and at his death, willed his collection of 700 books to the University of Massachusetts.

Living Heroes can offer inspiration, hope, and motivation to many at-risk students that may be bored, uncommitted or about to drop out of school. Says James McNamee, Catholic Diocese School Superintendent, "To keep children interested in learning and committed to excellence is the best tool we have to combat the problem of drug abuse and apathy in our society."

SCHOLARSHIP FUNDS AND THE HERO CONCEPT

by Rev. Dr. Robert P. Lawrence, Fall River, Massachusetts

One of the dramatic appeals for raising scholarship funds for aspiring students seeking a higher education is to encourage a donor to contribute a $2,000 scholarship in honor of, or in memory of a loved one. The recipient considers the person in whose name the scholarship is given a hero and a meaningful relationship is developed between the two parties. To associate the donor as a hero, apart from the financial benefits, is an educational process within itself whereby the donor as the hero is elevated in status, the student is assured an education, and our communities are assured talented future leadership.

In a day in which our value systems dictate that heroes are people who earn big incomes, it seems increasingly important that students reassess their beliefs about heroes and perceive that a real hero is one who is willing to make a financial commitment for a student's further education—by providing a scholarship for that student.

Through the American Dream Challenge, a young person comes to understand that the real heroes of life are those with concerns for a better society and stronger, as well as fulfilled, individuals. The hero is one who wants what is best for another person.

The word "hero" is a Greek word meaning "servant." The Greeks had a pantheon of hero demigods and gods from Achilles to Zeus. Through the centuries, the enduring heroes have been those who inculcate ideals, those who stir the human soul, those whose source of true power has been internal, and whose worth has been genuinely godly.

Somehow some of our young people have lost that concept of the real hero in their lives. Our contemporary concern is in recognizing the true hero, and the American Dream Challenge makes every effort to demonstrate to our youth that the real heroes today are those who want for them the power of a good education.

Carlyle, the Scottish essayist, held that "the history of the world is the history of its heroes" and the need to have heroes who are exemplary for our youth is the intent and purpose of the American Dream Challenge.

We identify ourselves with greatness when we have taken a stand for significance and when one can contribute something of themselves to make a difference in the lives of others—especially our youth. A nation without heroes is a nation without a future. The spirit of America from its very foundation has been the spirit of developing and fulfilling the promises of those who have the potential of accomplishing the ideals of the American Dream Challenge.

There is a true story from the autobiography of the noted educator, Booker T. Washington, in his book "Up From Slavery". He shares the exciting story of his pilgrimage from slavery to education and freedom. After the Civil War, the young man migrated with his family to Malden, West Virginia, where he worked in the mines and as a house servant. Encouraged by his thirst for knowledge and by an employer who saw the worth and value of one who had something to contribute to the betterment of life and who provided the necessary funds for his studies, he set out on foot from Malden to Hampton, Virginia—approximately 500 miles to attend school. He tells us that he arrived at Hampton Institute with three assets: a tremendous desire for an education, a willingness to work hard, and the fond memory of the former employer who supported his motivation. Out of the disadvantage of his earlier years, and by someone who had faith in his future accomplishments, Booker T. Washington came to be the person whose life benefited untold numbers of other students by ultimately being the founder of Tuskegee Institute in Macon County, Alabama, in 1881. Harvard conferred an honorary degree upon him in 1896, and Dartmouth College conferred an L.L.D. degree in 1901.

Without that unnamed employer who made all things possible for Booker T. Washington, he might have remained an unknown slave in the place of his birth. And so it is for our youth today who might also remain an unknown "slave" to life's indifference, mediocrity and complacency were it not for heroes stepping forth in their lives to give all the hopes and promises of a better day.

America needs real heroes, not just the ones we read about in our daily newspapers, but also those who are behind the scenes, and in a low-key, humble manner become a hero to some unknown child who has the potential for greatness.

There is an old Jewish proverb that says: "Four things come not back— the spoken word, the spent arrow, time past, and the neglected opportunity." Don't let any opportunity pass you by as a hero, for this may be your day to respond by the depth of your character, the richness of your talent, and the significance of your career. You may emerge from the masses as a real hero. May your biography read as one who made a difference in the life of some student.

There is a sign inside a nursery that reads: "The best time to plant a tree was 25 years ago." The American Dream Challenge encourages you in seeking the desire to be a hero to someone by adding the sign: "The second best time to plant a tree is today."

Do you want to build a better America? Do you want to make an investment that will pay tremendous dividends in the future? Do you realize that our greatest asset today is tomorrow's youth?

Then become a real hero to someone who is worth the price of an education. Become a member of the American Dream Challenge by contributing $2,000 and have your name added to the Honor Roll of truly great Americans who want the best for their country, the promise for some student, and the ultimate fulfillment for themselves.

After Living Heroes are chosen and contributions made towards perpetual scholarships, they are paired at random with Fall River's fourth grade classes. The role model receives copies of students' American Challenge essays describing the importance and value of an education, and students receive copies of the hero's inspiring life story. In Fall River, it could be the Catholic bishop, a school principal, or even Anne Pacheco.

Anne Pacheco left school at 16 to help support her family but was determined to make something of her life. She worked days and went to school at night for her high school equivalency degree, then enrolled in bank courses to capitalize on her math and finance skills. After working in banking, she switched to day care work while taking income tax courses on the side. Today, she is a qualified tax preparer.

Whatever it takes, a community must inspire and motivate students to have the same positive attitude as Sophara Yoeun, who came to Fall River from Cambodia in 1996 as a fourth grader knowing little English. She learned to write and speak well in Fall River schools, and still enjoys attending each day "because it is an adventure." By reading science or history, she says she can imagine being anyone or anything she wishes.

Focusing on the long-range goal of finishing school and achieving helps keep students safe and healthy, especially in at-risk communities. Less substance abuse caused by boredom or wrong role models can result in fewer school dropouts, and it can result in more desire to attend college. Less money spent on drugs and alcohol can mean more money available for college courses. This is where Unsung Heroes come in and play a compelling role in keeping students focused on their education and where it can take them.

Unsung Heroes

Who are the unsung heroes? They are parents, teachers, teacher aides, school administrators, bus drivers, crossing guards, librarians—people who play vital roles in raising children and keeping them safe and cared for during the day, but are often unrecognized and unappreciated. If it is true that it takes a village to raise a child, then it is important to bring hardworking persons out of the shadows and corners and into the forefront of students' attention.

Towards this goal, Fall River has run frequent newspaper letters to the editor praising unsung heroes. For instance, the article "Parents Deserve Praise for Raising Good Kids" appeared in the *Fall River Herald News* on June 15, 2000. It described how 14 parents were honored by the city's Magnet Education Program. Program director Odete Amaewlo, Ph.D., cited these parents as role models for going the extra mile to guide their children properly. Newspapers should routinely spotlight young entrepreneurs, teen athletes, and students who devote time to charity and community service.

One parent at the June ceremony was invited on a local WHTB radio show to talk about his own parental role. Peter Duarte is a single dad who drives a truck full time but is willing to put his personal social life on hold while he raises his daughter. The show host received many calls from listeners thanking Duarte for his commitment, and other parents have been recognized as well.

McCarrick School Principal Mary Whittaker singled out parents Mike and Nancy Mullen on May 1, 2000, for making sure their three sons "...came to school well prepared and with enthusiastic attitudes. Mike and Nancy enrich their children's lives with a broad spectrum of worthwhile and creative activities." Several years ago, for instance, the whole family pitched in to paint and decorate the school office. Mike also got a carpenter to make bookcases out of surplus lumber donated by a local business.

In the past, more children and young teens were raised in homes with extended families. They talked to and learned from aunts, uncles, and grandparents—folks with wisdom, life experience, and good advice. Now more and more relatives live far apart and young persons grow up in an adolescent vacuum. Young people see only other young persons who might have the same bad habits. Youth must be exposed to adults. It does take a whole village to raise a child, and to open up a wide world of choice and opportunity.

The time for teachers is now. Teaching is an honorable, rewarding profession to which students should aspire. The nation needs a new generation of teachers to replace those retiring or leaving school systems. Education and literacy has been a top concern of the last two presidents, many current governors, first ladies, and local officials. Teachers' salaries, benefits, and incentives have increased to bring the brightest prospects into the profession.

One does not have to tune into the annual Disney Teacher Awards to find talented classroom instructors. Search your own hometown. Fall River has recently recognized three exemplary teachers as unsung heroes and awarded them citations from the city, the city council, the school department, and the state senate.

Susan Lanyon, fourth grade teacher at the Wiley School, entered the profession 27 years ago to share her love of learning and to make a difference in children's lives. Her commitment has not diminished after all these years. She enthusiastically shares thoughts with her students about her own college education, fostering students' wishes and hopes. They brainstorm ideas for continuing their schooling and come up with good ones. "There are no losers in this essay contest. The writing alone produces thoughts never shared before," she says.

Denise Ward, acting principal of the Silvia School, is another believer in the American Dream Challenge." I try to instill in them that their education is a privilege that some people will never experience and to utilize it to the fullest," said Ward, who has won many education awards and appreciates the notes, letters, and gifts she receives from former students thanking her for her effort. "It makes my adrenaline level rise when I see the look of excitement in their eyes when they have successfully achieved a goal in school. That's what teaching is all about!" she beams.

"I was also privileged to be named one of three exemplary teachers and unsung heroes," continued Ward. "I started out in a business career, but I changed to teaching when I discovered that I had a flair for training and instructing new employees, demonstrating product use to consumers and writing technical material. My goal now is to mine wealth and riches from young minds and to turn students onto lifelong learning instead of earning a few cents off an inanimate store product. I want students to be able to think on their feet, speak and write clearly and effectively, and to enjoy doing it."

Choices

Our choices define us; we become the sum of our choices. The commitment and dedication of earning fast fame and fortune in a glamour field is not necessarily a bad choice or goal, and young persons are not wrong to want that. But it is vital that they understand and appreciate the incredible discipline and will power needed to achieve that goal. Take billionaire real estate developer Donald Trump, for instance. He lives a glamorous lifestyle and carves his name into palatial buildings. How many young persons, though, know he attended military school, learned discipline, was an athlete, and shuns alcohol because it can dull his mind and he always wants to perform to peak efficiency. These choices represent good values.

Choices are the third component of the American Dream Challenge. Realizing the potential rewards or consequences of choices can make vivid and even harsh impressions upon students. It raises student consciousness by leaps and bounds to see the grim reality of prison life that can await people who make poor choices in life and fall in with the wrong crowd.

Many of the choices young people face are highly influenced by the social setting of their school. That in mind, Fradkin began to appear at two to three local schools a week to talk to students about the dangers that await them if they abuse drugs, fall in with the wrong groups, pick up harmful habits, and make poor life choices. He pointed out that $30,000 to $100,000 a year is spent keeping a convict locked up, but, because there are so many prisoners nationwide, many have to be released to make room for others. This "revolving door" aspect of prison could be bolted and much criminal justice money reallocated to balancing budgets, strengthening city financial health, and keeping young people from dropping out of school and going to jail in the first place.

In January, 1998, Bristol County (Mass.) Sheriff Thomas M. Hodgson began to collaborate with Fradkin's American Dream Challenge to reach youngsters of the county with the message that those who stay in school are generally not going to wind up in his jail. "We believe that this is a program that can change the destiny of youngsters who are slogging around in the quicksand of despair, the surest route to a life of crime," said Hodgson.

As of mid-1997, one in every 155 U.S. residents was in jail, many for relatively minor drug and alcohol charges. Again, Fradkin and Hodgson emphasize the huge amounts of government money that could be saved and allocated to social and education programs. The enormous rise in imprisonment—early six percent in 1997, from 1.6 million to 1.7 million inmates—can be reversed, they believe.

Hodgson and Fradkin target the American Dream Challenge age group–grades four and five in elementary school and grades six through eight in middle school–with the Choices message. On December 9, 1997, the two community leaders spoke to sixth and seventh graders at Fall River's Morton Middle School about how bad choices can bring bad consequences, including loss of freedom and future. Hodgson selected three volunteers from the audience who were told to stand on a 7-by-10 foot block of paper for ten minutes to experience lock up. Then he asked them how they liked their jail cell. One said it was boring. Another complained that there was no TV.

The sheriff explained that there is no TV in the cells and added, "After school, you do your homework, talk on the phone, and play football. Things change in jail. Bad choices lead to waking up at seven every day, even on weekends, having no privacy, no walls, and not being able to call mom or dad. They lose all privileges and, if they want them back, they have to make good choices and know how to be a good citizen and a good person."

Hodgson admitted that most students would not end up in jail, but he cautioned them to remember that they are their country's greatest assets and they have the whole world in their hands if they take the time to learn, to understand, and to study.

A similar presentation was made to Kuss Middle School students in Fall River on January 7, 1998. The sheriff brought a 26-year-old former convict to talk to the students about his own poor choices. His mistakes started simply, he said, with marijuana use at 12, falling in with the wrong kids at middle school in order to be cool, cocaine use at 14, then knifepoint robberies to support his drug habit. He landed in jail for five and a half years.

Students asked him what he did in jail. "Nothing," the former convict said." I basically sat in a small jail cell with two other people, waiting to get a chance to go to the gym or to the prison yard. There's no television in the cells; there's nothing to do." The students looked very troubled by his comment. Then the sheriff drove the point home.

"Who likes poached eggs?" he asked the sixth and seventh graders. Only a few raised their hands. "Well, for those of you who like poached eggs, you're in luck. Because whatever they give you to eat in prison is what you get— whether you like it or not. It's all about making the right choices in life."

Since that first school presentation in late 1997, Fradkin and Hodgson have appeared at nearly every school in Fall River. The Bristol County Sheriff's Department have contacted the Massachusetts Sheriff's Association and the National Sheriff's Association in Virginia to publicize the effectiveness of these school presentations, and continue to send former convicts all over the county to talk to school assemblies, summer camps, detention camps, and other youth gatherings.

Rhode Island also has a technique to impress students, using the video "10 Seconds," a short teen awareness video made for the state attorney general's task force to prevent violence in schools. It forcibly demonstrates how quickly things can go wrong. For instance, it takes only ten seconds for a drunken teen to get into a car and start it. It takes only ten seconds for a teen to pick up and use a weapon to settle a dispute. This video was sent to every middle school, school district, and public library in Rhode Island.

Fradkin believes that programs like the American Dream Challenge that uphold role models, heroes, positive behavior, and the learned habit of making right choices can also reduce racism in our country." Their great value is that they unite and encourage a community to come together regardless of race, color, or creed," said Fradkin. "When people work together in motivating and supporting their greatest treasure— their children—they will work and understand one another with less prejudice. Children will see adults as a cohesive force against racism."

"I believe if you give our future leaders hope, opportunity, and a goal or a dream to look forward to, they will be more apt to shun vices and violence. The American Dream Challenge is such a program. When properly established, teachers are better appreciated and can reach students more effectively, making a difference in their lives, perhaps inspiring them, too, to become teachers."

It is of vital importance to keep innovating ways to reach and inspire students with hope and patience for the future. Temptations can distract and threaten them, even lead them down the road to ruin. Drugs are easily available to rich and poor alike in big cities, suburbs, and rural areas, and completely insidious in their destructiveness.

Fradkin has seen his dream expand from the Dollars for Scholars r in Fall River to the Citizens' Scholarship Foundation of America—which operates more than 1,100 chapters in 39 states and the District of Columbia, along with 172 ScholarShops. This is a far-reaching, positive vision for an 80-year-old man who is still vitally involved as an unpaid volunteer in the effort to make the American dream come true for many in our nation. Despite heart attacks, bouts with cancer, and hip operations, Fradkin still speaks out whenever and wherever possible.

"A garden properly nourished, fertilized and cared for will bear fruit and flowers. It is also true that students who are properly motivated, inspired, and given respect and credibility can be the ones who will stay in school, stay off drugs, alcohol and tobacco, avoid teen pregnancy, shun violence, and remain directed toward higher education."

After a long rewarding career as an optometrist, the son of poor Russian-Jewish immigrants who made his own dream come true—and thanks the country that made this dream happen—can truly say, "There is absolutely no end to what free-thinking people who believe in helping others can do. That, I think, is the true value of our grassroots do-it-yourself movement: giving people the idea, the dream, and letting them expand it, enlarge it, and put their own stamp on it all for the purpose of building a better America through education."

"So many times, I've been discouraged, and I've sometimes felt like Don Quixote chasing after the impossible dream. With all the negativism and crime in our country, I sometimes feel like we're shoveling sand against the tide."

"But America can be made better. I believe that, but only if people stop sticking their heads in the sand and stick their necks out, instead, to make this country a better place."

CHAPTER 15
A NEW EDUCATIONAL VISION FOR COMMUNITY RESPONSIBILITY

by Dr. William C. Nelsen, President,
Citizens' Scholarship Foundation of America

Since Dr. Irving Fradkin's autobiography was originally published in 1993, Citizens' Scholarship Foundation of America (CSFA) has continued to grow rapidly. The number of Dollars for Scholars chapters surpassed 1,100 in the year 2002.

More and more colleges and universities are recognizing the value of our work in mobilizing Americans for education. Consequently, our Collegiate Partner roster has grown to 445 and will continue to increase as the Dollars for Scholars program reaches new sections of the nation. As David Bach has outlined in his chapter, the ScholarShop program has been launched and has already reached 172 communities and neighborhoods.

Dollars for Scholars chapters have also been reaching youth at earlier ages to motivate and prepare them for postsecondary education through mentoring programs, parent workshops, and special programs, such as Dr. Fradkin's American Dream Challenge. CSFA's Scholarship Management Services currently administers more than 900 sponsored programs, primarily for corporations but also for foundations, community foundations, associations and individuals.

Throughout this continuing rapid growth of the organization, we have never strayed from the original philosophy that led Fradkin and other volunteers to establish the original "Dollars for Scholars" scholarship approach in Fall River, Massachusetts. This philosophy maintains that citizens must take responsibility for motivating, challenging, and assisting their local youth to obtain the critical benefits of education. People can act in a variety of ways to promote and ensure educational success, through community and neighborhood action, through corporate leadership and action, or by encouraging government to do its share.

Today, educators are realizing more than ever that educational achievement for our youth depends on the attitudes and actions of people in each local community. Despite the emergence of worldwide information systems, our young people still gain, or lose, their desire and expectations—for educational achievement primarily at the local level—from parents, teachers, student peers, and local community leaders. A community that is mobilized for education, that sets high expectations for its youth, that provides visible signs that it cares about educational values, will produce youth who are motivated to do well in school and aim to succeed in postsecondary education.

Thus, CSFA will continue to pursue an educational vision that is simple, yet powerful. That vision sees more and more local communities —rural, suburban, and inner city—being given the tools and resources to exercise their responsibilities for improving educational achievement. Dollars for Scholars, and early intervention programs like ScholarShop, American Dream Challenge, and communitywide mentoring programs represent excellent ways for communities to quickly gain such tools and resources.

But before we describe this new educational vision, we need to issue a series of warnings. I call these "Deceptions of the Day." These deceptions can lead people away from exercising their community educational responsibilities.

***Deception 1*—Postsecondary Education is not needed.** Those who create and push this deception point out that half of the nation's 132 million jobs don't require a college education. These people fail to point out that in this age of technology and information, virtually all students need some form of postsecondary education—in colleges, community college, or vocational schools. To be eligible for promotion to low and middle-level management positions, a Bachelors degree is increasingly necessary. In 1960, 40% of managers in corporations had Bachelors degrees and today, 80% have Bachelors degrees. Why? Employers value a college degree. It provides evidence that a person has learned to think, can adjust, and shows some discipline for hard work. As one employer stated, "The high school diploma no longer sends that message." In addition, the college graduate earns twice as much as those that do not have a college degree. The earnings gap between college education and non college-education adults has risen nearly 70% since 1980.

Even worse than the earnings gap is the knowledge or wisdom gap. The purpose of an education is not just to get a job, or a promotion, or earn more money. Education helps a person to understand, appreciate, and enjoy more of life and to tackle questions of meaning and values in life. An education enables a person to read well, write well, comprehend, solve problems, make better decisions, and be better able to help others, including one's own children. In my mind, it is not just bad policy or bad advice to say to young people that they don't need postsecondary education; it is a crime, especially when we convey this false message to low-income minority youth. To fail to raise educational expectations and to fail to demand more of minority youth is the highest form of prejudice. Do not be deceived! Our citizens must exercise their community responsibility to challenge and assist our youth to pursue postsecondary education.

Deception 2—**Government will now be able to take care of our college access problems.** In the late 1990's, we experienced a period of budget surplus for the federal government and many state governments. Many proposals on spending that surplus included support for college tuition and programs for preparation for college. For example, California doubled the size of the state's need-based student-aid program for students that have at least a "B" average, and other states undertook comparable initiatives. The deceivers will say that this trend means that there is no need for private sector support. What they fail to point out is that even lucrative grants don't cover living expenses and they don't reach the students who don't achieve a "B" average or don't keep the B average. These students also need assistance. In many states the need for student financial aid has actually increased, especially because of an increase in public and private higher educational costs.

Most importantly, we need to remind ourselves that state and federal legislation and appropriations can and will change. In the 1970s there was an increase in federal student aid, resulting in a substantial decrease in the sense of private and community responsibility. It was, in those years, much harder to create Dollars for Scholars chapters. Thus, when the need arose and public funding leveled off, we were not ready. Students suffered. The same can happen tomorrow. A different legislature, a different Congress, and a different economy will always come along. Indeed the initial years of our new century have been radically different economically than the late 1990's. Do not be deceived! Our citizens must exercise their community responsibility to challenge and give financial assistance to our youth from private resources as well.

Deception 3—**Money given to education experts will solve our education problems**. In recent years, billions have been spent by the federal government and major U.S. foundations and corporations on "educational reform" efforts and ideas. For example, in the past several years the Annenberg Foundation and local school districts spent $1 billion, including matched funds, on school reform. Recent studies show mixed results from those efforts. A high percentage of those funds were spent on high-priced consultants and educational think tanks. Federal reform monies often get lost in similar bureaucracy mazes. This waste of money is in direct contrast to the efficiency of CSFA, which uses 94 percent of the money it receives each year to directly benefit students through scholarships or educational support programs. For the fifth year in a row, *SmartMoney*, the *Wall Street Journal's* magazine of personal finance, has ranked CSFA as one of the 17 most efficient nonprofits in the country. *Worth Magazine* has also named CSFA as one of America's 100 best charities for 2001/2002. Money should be spent primarily directly on our youth or on the people who are not more than one person away from our youth, including teachers, mentors, parents, or youth-serving agencies. Do not be deceived! The next time a big amount is spent on "educational reform," we need to make sure it is helping people exercise their community responsibility to challenge and assist our youth.

Once we set aside these "deceptions of the day" we can then actively pursue a new vision of community responsibility in education. Our new vision is that citizens in every community—rural, suburban, or inner city, —will be mobilized to challenge and support all their youth to reach their educational potential. No youth should be neglected. No youth should be left behind.

What does it mean to mobilize a community? It means to form partnerships with schools, parents, service clubs, youth-serving agencies, including Dollars for Scholars and ScholarShops, churches, synagogues and mosques. It means adopting clear goals of achievement and support. In setting goals, communities should make use of the tools from the Search Institute's Healthy Communities Alliance and their 40 Assets of Youth, and the five promises of the America's Promise Organization. Every child must experience a mobilized community that sets high expectations for all of its youth.

What does this vision mean for CSFA? CSFA cannot carry out this total vision on its own, but we can and must do our part at all levels—local, regional, and national.

A new era of local growth. This new growth is both inward and outward. Inward growth means to challenge our Dollars for Scholars volunteers to reach more youth in their communities. Some Dollars for Scholars chapters raise enough funds to be able to give out scholarships to every local graduate. If some can do it, all can do it. Some ScholarShop sites are reaching not just 10 to 20 youth, but 100 youth week after week. If some can do it, all can do it.

Outward growth means radically increasing the number of Dollars for Scholars chapters and ScholarShop sites around the nation. As of July 2002, more than 1,100 Dollars for Scholars chapters are active. More than 170 new chapters were created this past year—that's one new chapter being established somewhere in America every two days. Our vision is to increase as rapidly as possible the number of chapters to reach a total of 2,000 throughout the country. ScholarShop is a new program, but has more than 172 sites. Think about the impact on youth if every Dollars for Scholars community also had a ScholarShop and every ScholarShop site had a Dollars for Scholars chapter. We must dedicate ourselves to a new vision of growth, both inward and outward.

A new era of regional service. This inward and outward growth must be aided by increasing the number of state and regional service organizations. Several years ago CSFA adopted a new model for increasing the number of Dollars for Scholars chapters and providing chapters with better and more direct service. State and regional Dollars for Scholars organizations are being created with their own boards and staff and the power and responsibility to charter and serve chapters in their areas. Eight chartered regions are already active and five additional states and regions are currently being developed. One great strength of this new model is the dedication of the volunteer regional board members. Hundreds of businesses, educational, and civic leaders from various state and regions are now active supporters of the Dollars for Scholars movement.

Investing in the creation of new Dollars for Scholars regional organizations is one of the best investments that corporate, foundation or individual donors can make. In respect to Dollars for Scholars start-up gifts or grants, we speak of the "Power of Ten." For example, Colonel Barney Oldfield made a gift to CSFA two years ago of $500,000 to found new Dollars for Scholars chapters in the state of Nebraska. That gift will soon provide more than $5,000,000 in new scholarship funding raised by new local chapters throughout the state. Similar results have already been documented in other regions throughout the country.

A new era of national service support. CSFA's national organization is currently working on exciting new services for our regions and for chapters and ScholarShop sites. ScholarShop is developing new online programs. New opportunities for national sponsorships, cause-related marketing and events fund-raising are also being created. In 1998, CSFA created and launched National Scholarship Month to celebrate what is already being done to help youth through scholarships and to challenge others to join with CSFA in motivating and assisting our youth through scholarships. ScholarShop will continue to grow through new national partnerships with the Boys and Girls Clubs, YMCAs and others. Scholarship Management Services will continue to assist hundreds of additional corporations, associations, and individuals that are willing to help youth through scholarship programs. The Families of Freedom Scholarship Fund®, for which CSFA raised more than $100 million to provide educational support for children and spouses of the September 11, 2001 attack on America, demonstrates the tremendous potential of private sector support. CSFA encourages communities, corporations, foundations, and others to become part of this national movement and the new educational vision for America.

A story of a race that took place several years ago at the Seattle, Washington, Special Olympics summarizes this new vision of collective responsibility. Nine contestants, all physically or mentally disabled, were gathered at the starting line for the 100-meter dash. The gun sounded and all started out as fast as they could trying to get to the finish line first. But one boy stumbled and fell and began to cry. Hearing his cry, the other eight contestants slowed down, stopped, and looked back at the boy. Instead of going on, they all came back and picked up the boy who had fallen, linked arms, and all crossed the finish line together. Everyone in the stadium stood and cheered for a long time. The remarkable incident is still discussed by those who witnessed it. Every one of those youth became a winner and a model for us to follow. Isn't this what community responsibility is all about? We are responsible to reach out, reach over, and reach back to help all youth realize their educational potential.

In 1958 a group of volunteers in Fall River, Massachusetts, led by Dr. Fradkin, recognized this opportunity and their citizen responsibility—and they acted. Today that same basic idea of civic responsibility in education is more powerful and more necessary than ever before.

"Our progress as a nation can be no swifter
than our progress in education."
—John F. Kennedy

CHAPTER 16
THE FAMILIES OF FREEDOM SCHOLARSHIP FUND®

by Reyna Morenoff and Robert Rave

September 11, 2001, has a permanence etched in our collective memory like few other dates in history that separate yesterday from today, and then from now. It is from these rarest of moments that people will forever be able to tell where they were and what they were doing when they first heard the news. And it is during these times that a nation's ability to help and heal ultimately prevails. In the aftermath of an initial helpless feeling, a resilient people sought and found ways to help each other.

On September 17, 2001, less than one week after the terrorist attack on America, the Families of Freedom Scholarship Fund® (the Fund) was launched by Citizens' Scholarship Foundation of America℠ (CSFA), along with Lumina Foundation for Education, a private, independent foundation that strives to help people achieve their potential by expanding access to an education beyond high school.

The Fund was created to provide education assistance for postsecondary education to financially needy dependents of those killed or permanently disabled as a result of the terrorist attacks on America. Specifically, the Fund benefits children and spouses of the victims, including airplane crew and passengers, World Trade Center and Pentagon workers and visitors, and relief workers, including firefighters, emergency medical personnel and law enforcement personnel.

CSFA has always maintained its principle that education is a vital stepping-stone to triumph over life's obstacles. In essence, the Fund was created to ensure that victims' families who may need financial assistance could realize their educational dreams.

On September 29, 2001, in an unprecedented pairing of former political rivals, former President Bill Clinton and former Senate Majority Leader Bob Dole became co-chairs of the Fund's campaign effort.

President Clinton stated, "The tragedy of September 11 left many young people without parents; young people who with a helping hand and the chance for a higher education will go on to great things. Young people who, with your help, might even go on to become President of the United States. I am honored to be working with Senator Dole on the Families of Freedom Scholarship Fund to make sure that all of the victims' families of this tragedy can get the education that they want and deserve."

Senator Dole echoed President Clinton's remarks, noting, "Americans have shown extraordinary generosity and caring in the weeks following the attacks. I am grateful that we can play some small part in helping ease the burden of the victims and their families. The children and spouses of firefighters and police officers, flight crews and passengers, World Trade Center and Pentagon workers—all of the victims of the attacks—have lost so much. We hope that this scholarship fund will help erase some of their doubts and fears about their future."

The Fund has received widespread support from the American people, from grassroots events to cause-related marketing campaigns to generous corporate gifts, enabling CSFA to achieve its goal to raise $100 million for the Fund in the fall of 2002, ensuring access to postsecondary education for families most impacted by September 11.

As of July 2002, donations have been received by more than 20,000 individuals, corporations, foundations, organizations and others. TMP Worldwide, headed by Andy McKelvey, provided important in-kind marketing and communication resources, including a public service announcement with Clinton and Dole, advertising and a call center for handling inquiries and other resources. Revé Entertainment, headed by Josselyne Herman, provided pro bono production of two PSAs—one featuring Josh Hartnett and Julia Stiles and another featuring Susan Sarandon. Young people in communities all across the country have banded together to raise awareness, morale and money to support the educational dreams of kids they don't even know.

In January 2002, CSFA began assisting eligible students enrolled or enrolling in qualified institutions, including accredited two-and four-year colleges, universities, or vocational-technical schools. Financial awards are based on a number of factors, including the size of the Fund, the number of eligible participants and the financial need of applicants. CSFA is drawing on extensive experience in scholarship distribution.

CSFA has conducted extensive outreach to create a database of potentially eligible participants. As the database is being developed, CSFA is contacting the families of victims to ensure that children learn about potential education assistance opportunities for postsecondary education. Outreach has included all available means, including print media, broadcast and Internet, plus cooperation with government agencies, a wide variety of nonprofit organizations, and colleges and universities throughout America.

To efficiently handle the financial management of the Fund, CSFA has established a highly qualified Fund investment committee composed of financiers and investment counselors who have more than 100 years of combined professional experience in financial management. These professionals serve as volunteers on CSFA's Board of Trustees and National Advisory Board. Additional financial experts will be added for long-term oversight of the Fund. One hundred percent of the principal received from contributions goes directly to aid dependents of September 11 victims.

The Fund will terminate as of December 31, 2030, or when CSFA's Board of Directors determines that the needs of the victims' dependents have been met or can be met with reasonable certainty with less than all of the assets of the Fund. At that time, the Board of Directors of CSFA may redirect any excess assets of the Fund to support other postsecondary education scholarship programs.

CSFA and the Citigroup Foundation were catalysts in the effort to simplify the scholarship application process for families most affected by September 11 by working with other leading scholarship providers and associated organizations to form the September 11 Scholarship Alliance (Alliance).

The Alliance serves as an information clearinghouse to help ensure that financial assistance for postsecondary education, such as college, university and vocational-technical schools, gets into the hands of those who need it most with minimal paperwork and frustration. A toll-free phone number, 1-877-862-0136, is available to initiate the registration process of all eligible families and to obtain application information. Scholarship information is also available online at www.scholarships911.org.

"This is a difficult time for these families, and we want to make sure that no one's educational dream is deferred due to the events on September 11," said Charles V. Raymond of the Citigroup Relief Fund, which has led the effort to form the Alliance. "We believe the 'September 11 Scholarship Alliance' will make a real difference in streamlining the financial assistance process and establishing a system that will serve these families for the next 25 years."

The Alliance has adopted a common registration database and scholarship application form that will be used by CSFA to identify those scholarships for which each applicant is eligible. CSFA will also manage the distribution of scholarships to applicants on behalf of nearly all Alliance scholarship providers.

"We have been very pleased to be an active partner from the beginning of this effort to ensure that the children and spouses of the victims of September 11 have access to a 'one-stop shop' for all the scholarships for which they may be eligible," said Dr. William C. Nelsen, CSFA president." The Alliance has turned what could have been a very complicated and frustrating process for these families into something much more manageable."

The Alliance also is collaborating to coordinate communications to families and reach out to other scholarship funds." Hopefully, over time, any entity that is providing scholarships to the families of the victims of September 11 will be connected to the Alliance in some way," Raymond said.

CSFA also has endeavored to reach out to eligible students currently enrolled in postsecondary institutions by sending scholarship information to colleges, universities and vocational schools throughout America.

ALLIANCE MEMBERS PROVIDING SCHOLARSHIP FUNDING INCLUDE:

Children's Aid Society
Citigroup Foundation/Citigroup Relief Fund
Citizens' Scholarship Foundation of America℠/Families of Freedom Scholarship Fund®
DaimlerChrysler Corporation Foundation/Help the Children Fund
Energy Companies/The Power of America Fund
Institute for International Education
International Youth Foundation
Polo Ralph Lauren Foundation/American Heroes Fund

ALLIANCE MEMBERS SERVING AS ADVISERS INCLUDE:
American Jewish World Service
Educational Testing Services
Federal Emergency Management Agency (FEMA)
Jack Kent Cooke Foundation
National Association of Student Financial Aid Administrators (NASFAA)
New York State Higher Education Services Corporation
Pace University
Safe Horizon
September 11th Fund
Silver Shield Foundation
Twin Towers Fund
United Negro College Fund

The Families of Freedom Scholarship Fund sparked a tremendous display of teamwork throughout CSFA. Virtually every department of the staff was involved. Board members stepped forward to assist in a variety of ways and represented CSFA at events throughout the country.

Since September 11, the definition of community responsibility has ascended to a new level. The success of the Families of Freedom Scholarship Fund has already provided an historic validation of CSFA's vision of education. The unprecedented support for the Fund demonstrated at the local, regional, national and even international levels signifies a growing awareness of the essential value of education in dealing with life's challenges.

Just as the contestants at the Special Olympics once linked arms to cross the finish line together, the world has, in a sense, linked arms to stride into a brighter future. Through the Families of Freedom Scholarship Fund, CSFA will continue to work towards its goals to insure that the victims of September 11 have an opportunity to excel despite their tragic losses.

CSFA has always stood for excellence through education. A young person's learning experience can enable him or her to succeed in life and career, to reach out across social, economic and racial divides, and to confront and change his or her view of society and the global community. By encouraging every young person's capacity to learn, we are opening him or her up to his or her fullest potential; building a thoughtful and sensitive person and empowering him or her to make positive contributions to society and the world.

All young people, regardless of their physical or cognitive abilities, race, or socio-economic status, benefit from regular and continued participation in the power, wonder and joy of learning. Education provides an ideal forum for those of widely divergent abilities and backgrounds to unite as a team bound by a common goal.

These dreams can be realized by making higher education more readily available to America's youth. These are the benefits to be gained from providing young people with educational assistance from the Families of Freedom Scholarship Fund. This is the significance to be gleaned from continuing to band together to support education so that children in future generations will have an opportunity to grow up in a world that is more aware. And, these are the sentiments so eloquently expressed by President John F. Kennedy: "Let us think of education as the means of developing our greatest abilities, because in each of us there is a private hope and dream which, fulfilled, can be translated into benefit for everyone and greater strength for our nation."

"A different world cannot be built by indifferent people."
—*Peter Marshall*

EPILOGUE: REFLECTIONS AND A PERSONAL CHALLENGE

I'm still amazed by the growth of CSFA. It still seems incredible that a simple idea has generated and helped so many people in so many ways, but that's exactly what has happened.

For many friends and for many people whom I've never met, CSFA has given their lives a purpose. In community after community, the program has enabled quality people to provide input and to offer ideas that have been so instrumental in the growth of CSFA.

I did not mind the inconvenience of air travel, seeing only airports and seldom having the opportunity to get to know chapter representatives well. Those irritations went with the obligation that I accepted as founder of CSFA.

My greatest sacrifice was the time away from my family, especially my lovely wife. Many a speaking engagement, having been made months in advance, conflicted with school events of my children in elementary and junior high right through high school.

I felt pretty sad and forlorn many times, being away while the kids wistfully observing both parents of many other children at these occasions. That sure did hurt!

I feel good when I hear them say, now, that they're certainly proud of "dear old dad" for all that he has done for his fellow man. In a way, that makes it all worthwhile.

I am also particularly thankful and glad to acknowledge that our past president Joe Phelan was able to interest and enroll such quality people to become part of and help in the growth of CSFA.

Each CSFA Board Chairman, Eugene Struckhoff, Brad Norris, Ed Lee, Ralph Seifert, Burt Knauft, Lloyd Brandt, and John Wedum Steve Putman, and Phyllis McGrath have contributed his own special gift to make CSFA the largest organization of its kind in the country.

What impresses me is not the fact that the program has become so big, but the dignity and true spirit of democracy that chapter leaders and staff have engendered in helping their own young people to attain a higher education.

I'm just so pleased that the great leadership of our past presidents, and especially the dedication of long-term leader Joe Phelan, has been passed on to our current president Bill Nelsen. This gifted and charismatic leader has continued the growth in so many new directions because of his ingenuity and dedication, ably assisted by his excellent staff including: Fred P. Vogel, Executive Vice President, Finance & Administration; Marilyn E. Rundell, Vice President, Scholarship Management Services; Linda L. Mahoney, Vice President, Strategic Alliances; Barbara E. Arnold, Vice President, Public Affairs & Communications; David L. Bach, Vice President, Community Programs; Douglas H. Scott, Vice President, Development; and Anne Cheney, Controller.

There is absolutely no end to what free-thinking people who believe in helping others can do. That, I think, is the true value of our grass roots do-it-yourself movement—giving people the idea, the dream, and letting them expand it, enlarge it, add their own, all in the whole purpose of building a better America through education.

So many times, I've been discouraged, and I've sometimes felt like Don Quixote chasing after the impossible dream. With all the negativism and crime in our country, which is played up on the media, I sometimes feel like we're shoveling sand against the tide.

America can be made better. I believe that, but only if people stop sticking their heads in the sand, and stick their necks out instead to make this country a better place.

How Can You Help?

The best thing Americans can do to help improve this country is to invest themselves in the future by helping others. You can volunteer, you can help start a new Dollars for Scholars chapter or give time and energy to the chapter already active in your community, and you can make a financial contribution to Citizens' Scholarship Foundation of America. By supporting this tax-exempt, nonprofit, do-it-yourself, grass roots, democratic movement, you can help make this concept available to every community and state in our Union.

CSFA is certainly not the only answer to our nation's problems. But it is one of the answers. I challenge you to get involved, to contribute, and to say "yes" to the future of our young people—to the future of our nation.

ABOUT THE AUTHOR

Dr. Irving A. Fradkin, the son of Russian, Jewish immigrants, was born March 28, 1921 in Chelsea, Massachusetts. Fradkin attended the Massachusetts College of Optometry in Boston. In 1943, with $700 borrowed from his father, he opened his first office in Fall River, Mass., and continues to practice there today.

Fradkin ran for the Fall River school board in 1957 and lost. His platform contained the vision of community supported scholarships for local students. "If everyone in this city gave a dollar," he reflected, "a great deal could be done to help." Despite his school board loss, he decided to go ahead and seek local support for his idea. Fall River citizens responded by providing $4,500 and awarded 24 scholarships to local young people in 1958. This was the beginning of "Dollars for Scholars" community scholarship foundations. Fradkin's grassroots "Dollars for Scholars" program spread to 11 cities by 1961. These 11 communities joined together and incorporated as Citizens' Scholarship Foundation of America. Fradkin's one-man effort became a national organization. And Fradkin became a celebrity. He was written about in *Time* and *Reader's Digest*, received letters of commendation from presidents, and appeared on network television programs. Inquiries came from communities nationwide interested in starting a Dollars for Scholars chapter.

Thirty five years since CSFA beginnings, Fradkin is still dedicated to aiding students obtain higher education, for he believes that these students are the foundation for a better America. He estimates that he has traveled the equivalent of six times around the world drumming up support for students from those who support them best—their communities. Today there are over 650 Dollars for Scholars chapters, and CSFA has expanded its services to include the design and management of scholarship programs for corporations, foundations, associations, and individuals. Fradkin has never earned a penny from his obsession, yet he says, "I have all the riches a man could want. This is just my way of saying thanks for living here."

The following is a list of some of his many areas of service and of the ways in which he has been recognized:

Select List of Citations

National Giraffe Award, for "sticking his neck out," 1988
Paul Harris Fellow, Rotary Club, 1988

Algonquian Camp Fire Council, Honorary Life Membership, 1987
Indiana Sagamore of the Wabash, 1987 (Indiana's highest award)
Society for the Prevention of Blindness, "Man of Vision," 1986
Task Force of Private Sector Initiatives, 1983
Massachusetts Optometrist of the Year, 1982
Freedom Foundations Award, Action in Education, 1961 and 1971
State of Israel Bonds, "Man of the Year," 1976
Jewish War Veterans "Man of the Year," 1974

Merit in Education, Knights of Pythias, 1966
B'nai B'rith "Man of the Year," Fitchburg, Massachusetts, 1963
Honorary keys to six cites:
Coral Gables, Florida
Biddleford, Maine
Waterville, Maine
Dover, New Hampshire
Mankato, Minnesota
Fall River, Massachusetts

Civic Involvement

Co-Founder of Interfaith Brotherhood Council, Fall River, Mass., 1980
Chair. Emeritus of Citizens' Scholarship Foundation of America, Inc., 1980
Area Coordinator of the Nat'l Conference of Christians and Jews, 1976-78
Chairman of the State of Israel Bonds, 1976-77
Vice President of the United Jewish Appeal, 1975-76
Chairman of Civic Activities Committee, Lions Club, 1973-74

Biographies

Community Leaders and Noteworthy Americans, American Biographical Institute
Men of Achievement, Intrn'l Biographic Center, Cambridge, England
Encyclopedia Judaica
Who's Who in Religion
Who's Who in America
Who's Who in Massachusetts
International *Who's Who in Community Service*
Who's Who in World Jewry

Personal

Dr. Fradkin is married to the former Charlotte Sheinfield and has three children and three grandchildren.

Several of the awards listed previously deserve special mention:

Sagamore of the Wabash–1987

The Governor of Indiana confers the title "Sagamore of the Wabash" on those people who have performed distinguished service to the state. The name comes from the Indian lesser chief or wise counselor who would give advice to the chief. Those so named become a chieftain on the Governor's staff, with the title of Sagamore of the Wabash.

When Dr. Fradkin received the award, he reminded the young people who were present, "People are the heart and soul of America. When people receive scholarship help, they tend to realize their responsibility to help others. CSF has grown through this dynamic chain reaction. Your whole life changes when you have an education. You can do so much more for yourselves and your families."

Paul Harris Fellow–1988

The Paul Harris Fellow is the Rotary Club's most prestigious award and is named for the organization's founder. When Dr. Fradkin received the honor from the Rotary Club of Greater Fall River, Massachusetts, only two non-Rotarians in the area had ever received the award.

"It is people like you that make a better community, state and country," he told the group, "The dream of CSF is to try to motivate and inspire the future leaders of this country. If we work together, we will see what the private sector, public sector and industry can do. We can make a better world."

Giraffe Project Award–1989

The Giraffe Project is a national organization that seeks out and honors people who stick their necks out to make life better for others.

"People too often stick their heads in the sand and say, 'Why bother? What can I do to change anything?" Dr. Fradkin said when accepting the award, "In a democracy, what people can do, they should do. CSFA, which emphasizes that recipients have a moral obligation to give back through volunteer and financial support so other students will have a chance at education, embodies that principle."

Washington Medal–1990

The Freedoms Foundation, based in Valley Forge, Pennsylvania awards the Washington Medal to individuals, foundations, and corporations in an effort to help Americans become informed and active participants in the nation's political and economic life.

Upon receiving this prestigious award, Dr. Fradkin stated: "I share this award with all the countless volunteers across the nation who have made the program the success it is."

ABOUT THE COLLABORATOR

Michael J. Vieira is a teacher, freelance writer, and editor, living in Swansea, Massachusetts. Michael holds both the Bachelor of Arts and Masters of Arts degrees in English from Bridgewater State Teachers College, and a certificate of Advanced Study from Rhode Island College.

He has served as a writer for the New Bedford Standard-Times and the Providence Journal-Bulletin. He has published articles in Business Digest, Arts and Entertainment Magazine, and English Journal. He researched, wrote, and edited In Print: 100 Years of Student Journalism, a book concerning high school publications in Fall River, Massachusetts.

Since 1978, Mr. Vieira has served as a teacher of English and Journalism and Publications Advisor at B.M.C. Durfee High School in Fall River. He is also an Instructor of Technical Writing at Roger Williams College in Rhode Island.

"We, the people of the United States, in order to form a more perfect union, establish justice, insure domestic tranquility, provide for the common defense, promote the general welfare, and secure the blessings of liberty to ourselves and our posterity, do ordain and establish a Constitution for the United States of America."
—*The United States Constitution*

APPENDIX A

Excerpts From Dr. Fradkin's Speeches

"America — the land of the free! Forever? Not necessarily. Only so long as we maintain and strengthen our doctrines of freedom and human understanding can we continue to enjoy our freedom. Those doctrines will exist as long as our young people develop into leaders in government, professions, and business; through education to the extent each is capable.

"The Citizens' Scholarships Foundation is a catalyst equipped to assist in this desired result. Through the efforts and contributions of many, designed to afford our young people the education that our nation and our community desires them to have, this important program is made possible.

"The future of America is in your hands. You can only serve that future if you prepare yourselves for it. No matter what avenue you travel in pursuing your education, as long as you travel it with purpose and determination, you will reach the success, which will help make you a credit to yourself and to those with whom you come in contact.

"These scholarships are not gratuitous. They are repaid through your efforts and the results you achieve in your future lives."

—Waterloo, Iowa 1965

"Education and scholarships, generally speaking, are misunderstood. Neither is an end unto itself. In a democracy, there is no reason to award scholarships and educate deserving students unless they can be inspired and motivated to use their education not only for themselves, but also for the betterment of the community and country.

"Our priceless heritage of freedom and democracy can only be preserved by an educated citizenry devoted and inspired to use its principles and ideals. One who is fortunate enough to be educated in our country has a great moral obligation to use this education for the betterment of his fellow citizens.

"Our program is aimed at instilling in the scholarship recipients a deep-rooted desire to use their education not only to increase their own economic and social status, but to build a better community and a better America.

"Love for community and country is stronger when one works successfully to solve his or her own problems as an individual and as part of a community. A democracy can wither and die if all problems are left to solution by the government."

—Fall River, Mass.

"If you understand anything about a democracy, you must understand that if you relinquish 'of the people, by the people, and for the people' especially if you relinquish 'by the people' you've lost your democracy.

"Citizens' Scholarship Foundation is the last bastion, as I see it, against the government saying 'people are no longer interested in doing anything for themselves so we're going to make education available to everybody. We're going to give everybody loans. We're going to give everybody scholarships.'

"You're going to relinquish the freedom you do have if you're going to allow the government to do everything for you. This is not to say we do not need government aid — but that is not enough. It must be supplemented and augmented by people's own efforts in order to make education meaningful — to give motivation and inspiration.

"This CSF can do. We can give something of ourselves, and if we, the volunteers, can give something of ourselves to the future of the country, we're going to have a better country."

—Wheaton College

"This country has the potential to be a Mecca for everyone, but only if we who are living here understand that we have a responsibility to each other. "We are capable of changing this country, capable of taking it back, and capable of saying to our young children in schools: 'It is a privilege to go to school. You have to accept this as a privilege. You cannot take this opportunity to destroy that privilege for others.' If we ever did a thing like that, I tell you there would be a change in the school system.

"In a democracy, we, who have had so much more knowledge and so much more understanding, have to convey this sense that education is a privilege to the children. But we can only do this if we, ourselves, value education.

"It's not the gold in the ground that's valuable. It's the minds of these young people, because if these can be molded, they can be inspired to not only better themselves but to do something good for their neighbors and for their country."

—Mansfield, Mass.

"You wonder why I do what I am doing? I am sure that my story could be duplicated by many people who have come up the hard way, here and everywhere. We motivate and inspire these people who are successful. They say they did it themselves, but they couldn't do it themselves. They were able to do it because someone helped them along the way.

"If these people who have already received scholarships in the past could say, 'Finally, it's my turn to help somebody else' —if we could generate this feeling of 'I have been helped, let me help somebody else' — we will eventually build a better community. If we build a better community, it is a better country."

—Johnson & Wales University, RI

"When this plan, which was first called the Fall River Plan, started to unfold, I was told, 'It's impossible. You'll need an army to enroll the people.' But there were others whose letters and support spurred me on.

"It has not been easy. So many times, we almost went under, because of a lack of funds. Through it all, Charlotte and I were so sure that not only would CSF revolutionize scholarships, but the end result would give us an opportunity seldom given to ordinary citizens: to help build a better and more purposeful America through education. We willingly spent, over 26 years, literally tens of thousands of dollars out of our pocket, plus we invested untold hours even while I underwent hip operations.

"After the first several years of success, I saw this not only as a scholarship program, but as a chance to do service for my country by giving our greatest assets, the minds of our young people which are the future of this country, a chance for higher education.

"I believe Aristotle said it best, `All who have meditated on the art of governing mankind have been convinced that the fate of empires depends on the education of youth.'"

—St. Peter, Minnesota

"Any and every community in America can be enriched as a chapter of CSFA. Properly instituted, it will give back to the community and the individuals the dignity and privilege of influencing our future leaders.

'It is the dream and purpose of CSFA that the individual will be inspired and motivated to give something back to the community and better understand the need to perpetuate our priceless gifts of freedom and democracy."

—Claremont, New Hampshire

"CSFA can get at the heart of the young people and inspire these young persons to know that this is a democracy and that a democracy, regardless of its faults, is the best form of government and this is the greatest country that we have ever seen in the history of the world.

"Right now, in your city, is the best example of democracy because there is no other country in the world that gives scholarships away to average people. They'll give you a scholarship in Russia or in England if you're a top student and they have a reason to give it to you. They're going to channel you in a direction they want.

"But in America, it's different. We know that every one has a God-given ability, but what that ability is, nobody knows.

"You know, President Eisenhower and President Kennedy were average students. Einstein was an average student — in fact, he almost flunked out of school. Churchill was an average student.

"Nobody knows what ability one has until he or she can be motivated. This is what I can see, because I don't know which one of you young people is going to discover the cure for cancer or become the president of the United States or take the place of this great mayor here.

"You have the ability to go wherever you want because there is no end to what we, in this country, can do if we put our minds to it. The Citizens' Scholarship Foundation proudly seems to be the help you have in that direction."

—Lancaster, Pennsylvania

"The future of CSFA is exceedingly bright. We can be in a position to actually change the history of our country. Certainly, it can't be disputed that we have changed the lives of many thousands of young people by giving them an opportunity for higher education.

"Who knows which of these young people, who have been helped or who will be helped, will be the discoverer of cures for many diseases? Who knows which ones will be heads of government, be it city, state or country?

"We are in a position to influence, to inspire and to motivate the most dynamic and important assets in our country: our future leaders...

"If these students were sent letters of inspiration about the wonders and opportunities in our country, by local and national dignitaries along with each scholarship check, and if these letters were shared with all the recipients' classmates, we would have the potential of touching the lives of about a half-million students.

"Some of these students will read, share, and be affected. Some will ignore them. However, those that are inspired and motivated will remember that their neighbors helped them, and that only in America are neighbors willing and ready to help each other in true CSF manner.

"If these young people are, in turn, willing to share themselves, after achieving some success in their chosen careers, in their own communities, wouldn't it make for a better community, in turn making a better state, and again in turn, making a better America?"

—White River Junction, Vermont

"I believe the time is ripe for a re-evaluation of America's purpose and dreams. Why should the youth want to do something worthwhile with their lives, when there is nothing on the horizon to stimulate, motivate and inspire them?

"Multi-millions of dollars are spent to sell products successfully, such as beer, cars, cosmetics, etc. Why not advertise and promote the most important product we have here in America — our priceless freedom and democracy and the valuable people who are doing something to better it?"

—Bloomfield, Connecticut

"I used to think that there was no God. As a college student and young adult, I would argue, 'If there is a God, why would he allow all this evil?'

"When Marlene, our first child, was born, then I realized the miracle of creation. When I marveled on that tiny baby, so complete yet so small, I began to believe in God.

"Some believe life evolved from a single cell. How could a single cell develop into the magnificent temple that is the human body?

"Greater thinkers than I have debated the issue of God for centuries, but I have come to grips with it by looking at the human body. Who else but God could have conceived such a marvelous machine?

"Look at the brain. It is small, yet the largest computer has not been able to duplicate its function.

"Look at the heart. It is only the size of a fist, yet it pumps more than 4200 times an hour, pushing five quarts of blood per minute through our veins, and providing enough energy to lift one and a half tons a foot high off the ground.

"The whole body proves to me that whatever made us, made us magnificently. With a circulation system that pumps year after year, and a brain that processes millions of pieces of information.

"It's also incredible that no matter where we came from or what color we are on the outside, inside we are all alike. The heart, the kidney, and the rest of the organs are all the same.

"Even the blood is the same. Nobody can tell from the color of the blood whether you came from Africa or Israel.

"There has got to be a purpose for life. Is it just to drift and wander? No. Whoever made us made us for a reason — and that has to be to help make this world a better place to live.

"There is greatness in all of us, and that's what I see in Citizens' Scholarship Foundation. CSF can give to every person an education, which will translate not into making money, but to an opportunity to help others. If people would only do that, we could make this country a better place to live."

—Johnson and Wales University, Providence RI

"How do we measure success in this country? Money is not the answer. It is people who make the difference. Money will not bring about a better community or country, nor will it create all the necessary jobs or community pride. Even the scholarship money, which we provide, will do little to help improve this country if we cannot awaken the spirit of America in our young people.

"What is the good of merely giving out money, if those receiving it are not inspired to use it to appreciate our priceless freedom and democracy? As long as the media is bombarding our minds with violence and all forms of garbage, a better society will simply never happen, regardless of any amount of money given.

"There must be a renewal and a re-awakening of our basic values. After more than 200 years, I believe America's greatest assets still can be found in the dream of democracy, in the creation of our country, and in the sharing of our priceless freedom.

"Why did our parents and grandparents emigrate to the United States in the first place? They came to this country to improve themselves, and to provide a better life for their children and grandchildren.

"But they did not expect a free ride—they came willing to work to improve their situation, and to make this country better. Just like our forefathers, our goal also must be: 'How can I help to develop a better neighborhood, community, and/or country?'

"This lesson is often lost on our children. I wonder if the young people would ever try to imagine what would have happened to them if their parents or grandparents had remained in their native lands. Civil wars are raging unceasingly in Africa, Europe, Asia, and all over the world. Death, destruction, starvation, AIDS, and many other diseases, no schools, no education, no hope, and even worse could have likewise been the destiny of all of us.

"Many of our young people today would not have been born, would have died in infancy or would have been victims of horrible diseases or instruments of destruction if their parents or grandparents had not come to the U.S.

"This is the lesson we have to keep alive: America is a blessed country, but only if we work and strive to keep it so. Democracy, like money, does not guarantee complete happiness and success, but offers the best opportunity and hope to make a better life."

—Student Body, B.M.C.
Durfee High School, Fall River, Massachusetts

"When we first got married, there was a time I said to my wife, 'What did you want to buy a $1.98 blouse for?'

"It wasn't that I didn't want her to have it. We just couldn't afford it. Now, because we've worked, we've saved, she is able to buy all the $1.98 blouses– if there were such a thing–that we want.

"You see, I've got everything you can offer a person. Money is not my God. Money is not something that I had an abundance of, but I have much more than money. I have the love of my wife, my three great children and my three marvelous grandchildren.

"This is something that nobody can put a value on. I know I'm a lucky person, but I also know that, because I'm so fortunate, that I've got to give something back.

"That, I think is the only way we can make America better. By educating our young people, not just in order to make money, but to learn the value of giving and sharing. Citizens' Scholarship Foundation provides that example."

— Bristol Community College,
Fall River, Mass.

"When the Athenians finally wanted not to give to society, but for society to give to them—when the freedom they wished for most was freedom from responsibility—then Athens ceased to be free."

—Edward Gibbon, Historian

APPENDIX B

Endorsements of Dr. Fradkin and Citizens' Scholarship Foundation of America

Endorsements

The Citizens' Scholarship Foundation and I have been fortunate to receive some kind words in editorials from various newspapers and in letters of support from people in all walks of life. The following provide a glimpse into the support that this program has generated.

"Your work to expand the educational opportunities among our young people addresses one of the most difficult challenges we face as a nation today. Your commitment to this cause and your determination to succeed will have a helpful and positive impact.

"I commend you for your willingness to become involved in the lives of others. Your example imparts a sense of our responsibility for our fellow countrymen."

—President George W. Bush, 1990

"When a community does something like this (Citizens' Scholarship Foundation), it shows there is an interest in the well being of their youth and that's the kind of place that people will want to raise their children and ultimately will stimulate the town."

—Ruth Hickerson, donor, Brooklyn, Iowa, 1990

"Created in response to the increasing cost of higher education and the financial obstacle this oftentimes poses, this initiative is about people helping people, neighbors helping neighbors, and private citizens' helping each other. I commend the various local community-based groups for endeavoring to establish a source of financial assistance for scholars who wish to attend institutions of higher education."

—Senator Dan Quayle, 1986

"The notion underlying the Citizens' Scholarship Foundation is the importance of grass roots contributions to make it possible for students from one's own home town to receive higher education. The way the Foundation has spread is proof of just how sound that original notion was."

— *Fall River Herald News*, 1981

"Many people talk about the need to help others, to improve educational opportunity in this country, and to demonstrate to young people that there are people in society who care about them. Very few people have put these sentiments into effect with anything like the vigor and benefit of Dr. Irving Fradkin."

—Representative Barney Frank of Massachusetts

"The aid Citizens' Scholarship Foundation brings to communities throughout the country in setting up scholarship programs for local students provides an invaluable service in furthering the educational development of our nation. Your efforts reflect the best in the American spirit of concern for our fellow citizens and the future of our nation."

—President Ronald Reagan, 1981

"The philosophy has been to award as many small scholarships as possible rather than fewer ones for large sums of money ... and to impress on the students that the help wasn't coming from some giant give-away program in the sky, but from their own neighbors. Those who got the aid were told they had a moral obligation to repay it, so that others could be helped...That...was democracy in action."

—Boston Herald American, 1981

"The dollars provided by Citizens' Scholarship Foundation, and this expressing of care, means a great deal to many students. You are having a significant impact on the lives of students students who otherwise might not attend college or might have to delay their higher education plans."

—President John E. Worthen,
Ball State University, Muncie, Indiana

"The Citizens' Scholarship Foundation invests in the most important resource in America — our youth. All of our futures depend on how our youth will cope with the challenges in the 1990's and the 21st century. Their education is important to us all. I commend the Citizens' Scholarship Foundation for their work and dedication in offering the opportunity for young students to get the education they need."

—Congressman Dan Burton, 1985

"It's simple. We want to enhance educational opportunities for young people. CSFA's professionalism, knowledge, and responsiveness helped us do that."

—M. Ray Haase, Vice President,
Tultex Corporation, Martinsville, Virginia

"The time is both right and ripe for the creation of Dollars for Scholars Chapters in school districts all over the United States. No matter what one's views of the current state of education, it is clear that Americans must be better educated and more skilled five and ten years hence than at any point in our nation's history. For many, that means going on to college after high school for everyone, it means a higher level of education...

"In rural America, in earlier centuries, communities got together to help raise a new barn. It brought the community together and was a great help to the individual farmer. Dollars for Scholars brings out those same feelings and energies and provides the same kind of benefits both to the individual and to the community as a whole. No one loses and everyone gains."

—John E. Bierwirth, Superintendent,
Portland Public Schools

"The reality of ordinary citizens and neighbors contributing to the higher education of young people through personal private giving should be a tenet of education. Although for many years, thousands of students have been helped by CSFA, the greater potential of Irv Fradkin's Dollars for Scholars chapters is yet to be realized. There is much work to be done in the inner-city, the rural south, and the vast regions of the west for all students including African-Americans, Hispanics, and First Americans.

"Indeed, as founder of a local chapter in an inner-city high school, I am encouraged by our first four years of private giving. More than a hundred high school graduates have received awards to further their education.

I feel such golden opportunities duplicated across the country are a direct link to all our tomorrows."

—Marquita McLean, Cincinnati, Ohio
Local Dollars for Scholars chapter founder
and CSFA Governing Trustee

"I remember your idea of uniting the people of Fall River and, with small sums of money from each, raising enough money to help your high school students further their education. It sounded great but impossible, and I was not the only one to tell you so—was I? But you did and the 'Dollars for Scholars' program was born.

"Then you started talking about other communities having their own CSF programs. I remember saying, and I was not the only one, that nobody else but you would put in the time and effort necessary to accomplish it.

"But as you kept talking about it, I decided to see what would happen in Pittsfield. It took me about a year and we, too, succeeded. And it was easier for me because I could show my people what was happening in Fall River.

"What I hadn't realized at the time was that the need was so great and the idea so powerful that people needed an opportunity to participate and once the community was involved, our American industry could be counted on.

"Now your scholarship program grows and grows and where it ends nobody knows. Awesome!"

— Dr. William Fradkin, Optometrist,
Las Vegas, Nevada (former president, Pittsfield
Dollars for Scholars Chapter, Massachusetts)

APPENDIX C

Dollars for Scholars® Chapter List
(1,117 Chapters as of 8/28/02)

ALABAMA (1)
Wil-Low Dollars for Scholars (Hayneville)

ARIZONA (2)
North Canyon Area Dollars for Scholars (Phoenix)
CSF of Tucson-Habbjach

CALIFORNIA (54)
All Are Achievers (AAA) Dollars for Scholars (Inglewood)
Alpha Phi Alpha Dollars for Scholars (Los Angeles)
CSF of Banning
COBA Dollars for Scholars (Los Angeles)
Carrol Alice Stout Scholarship Foundation (El Cajon)
Castle Park Alumni Dollars for Scholars (Chula Vista)
Century Dollars for Scholars (SantaAna)
City Club Foundation (San Francisco)
City of Commerce Dollars for Scholars
Community Scholarship Association of Anaheim UHSD
Crenshaw High School Dollars for Scholars
New Media Academy Achievement Foundation (Los Angeles)
Crenshaw High School Scholarship Foundation (Los Angeles)
EDU Dollars for Scholars (Los Angeles)
Eagle Rock High School Scholarship Foundation (Los Angeles)
Echo Park Boys & Girls Club Dollars for Scholars (Los Angeles)
Esperanza Scholarship Foundation Dollars for Scholars (Ontario)
F.G.B.C. Community Development Corporation (Los Angeles)
Farmers Fair Dollars for Scholars (Perris)
Farmersville Dollars for Scholars
Fostering Opportunities Dollars for Scholars (San Diego)
CSF of Fullerton UHSD
Duane E. Furman High School Scholarship Foundation (Madera)
Garfield High School Alumni Dollars for Scholars (Los Angeles)
Glenn County Scholarship Foundation (Willows)
John Glenn High School Dollars for Scholars (Norwalk)
Gompers AVID Dollars for Scholars (San Diego)
Greater Riverside Dollars for Scholars
Hispanic Chamber of Commerce of Orange County Dollars for Scholars (Santa Ana)
Hoover High School Dollars for Scholars (San Diego)
La Costa Canyon High School Dollars for Scholars
Laguna Beach High School Scholarship Foundation
Dollars for Scholars, Lincoln Heights (Los Angeles)
Linda Vista Dollars for Scholars (San Diego)
Los Angeles County Court Schools Dollars for Scholars
Murrieta Valley High SchoolScholarship Foundation New Vision Scholars (Bellflower)
Nurturing Inspired Achievement (Los Angeles)

Oakland's Advance A Student ScholarshipFund
Ocean Beach Dollars for Scholars
Oroville Educational Foundation
Paloma Valley High School Dollars for Scholars (Menifee)
Petaluma Educational Foundation
Ramona High Dollars for Scholars
San Bernardino Community Scholarship Association
San Diego County Court Schools Scholarship Foundation
Santa Ana High School Dollars for Scholars
Star Achievers Dollars for Scholars (Long Beach)
CSF of Temecula
Torrey Pines Dollars for Scholars Foundation (Leucadia)
Tustin Women In Chambers of Commerce Dollars for Scholars
Valley High School Scholarship Foundation (Santa Ana)
Ward AME Church-A.W. Jordan W.M.S. (Los Angeles)
Wilmington Dollars for Scholars
Woodlake High School Foundation Dollars for Scholars

COLORADO (1)
CSF of Fountain-Fort Carson and Widefield High Schools

CONNECTICUT (22)
CSF of Avon
CSF of Bloomfield
CSF of Canton
CONNCAP Dollars for Scholars (New Britain)
Coventry Scholarship Foundation
Ellington Community Scholarship Association
Greater Hartford Interracial Scholarship Fund
Hord Foundation, Inc. (Danbury)
Manchester Scholarship Foundation,Inc.
Norwalk Mentor Program Scholarship Fund
Rippowam Dollars for Scholars (Stamford)
CSF of South Windsor
CSF of Stafford Springs
Torrington Area Foundation for Public Giving
CSF of Washington
Waterbury Foundation
Wesleyan University Upward Bound Parents Advisory Group (Middletown)
CSF of Wethersfield
Willington Scholarship Foundation-PTA
Windham Dollars for Scholars (Willimantic)
Windsor Locks Dollars for Scholars
The Woodbury Scholarship Fund

DISTRICT OF COLUMBIA (2)
Calvin Coolidge Alumni Association
CSF of Simpson-Hamline UMC

FLORIDA (3)
The Brevard Schools Foundation (Melbourne)
CSF of Indian River County (Vero Beach)
Lake Worth Dollars for Scholars Foundation

GEORGIA (5)
Beulah Enrichment & Resource Center Dollars for Scholars
Carnel Cook Memorial Dollars for Scholars (Atlanta)
Grambling State University Alumni Association of Metropolitan Atlanta
Edmond T. Kemp Seeds of Promise Dollars for Scholars (Atlanta)
South Fulton Dollars for Scholars (College Park)

IDAHO (3)
Castleford Citizens' Scholarship Foundation

Gooding Academic Boosters Dollars for Scholars Foundation, Inc.
Wood River Valley Dollars for Scholars Foundation (Blaine County)

ILLINOIS (142)
AACM Dollars for Scholars Fund (Chicago)
Antioch Chamber of Commerce & Industry Dollars for Scholars
Bartlett Lions Club Dollars for Scholars
Beecher Community Scholarship Association
Broadview Youth Outreach Alliance
Burbank Chamber of Commerce Dollars for Scholars
Burlington Lions Club Dollars for Scholars
CCC Dollars for Scholars Fund (Chicago)
C-U One-To-One Mentoring Scholarship Foundation, a Dollars for Scholars Chapter (Champaign)
Cardunal Chamber Women's Council Dollars for Scholars
Carroll County Farm Bureau Foundation (Mt. Carroll)
Carthage School District Foundation
Cary-Grove High School Booster Club
Chenoa Crossroads Club Dollars for Scholars
Chicago Academy's Dollars for Scholars
Chicago Education Alliance Dollars for Scholars
Chicago Heights Kiwanis Dollars for Scholars
Chicago Public Schools (Central Office) Dollars for Scholars
Chicago Public Schools (Region 1) Dollars for Scholars
Chicago Public Schools (Region 2) Dollars for Scholars
Chicago Public Schools (Region 3) Dollars for Scholars
Chicago Public Schools (Region 4) Dollars for Scholars
Chicago Public Schools (Region 5) Dollars for Scholars
Chicago Public Schools (Region 6) Dollars for Scholars
Cissna Park Education Foundation
City of Palos Hills Dollars for Scholars
Country Club Hills Chamber of Commerce Dollars for Scholars
Crescent Iroquois Boosters Club Dollars for Scholars (Crescent City)
DBR Chamber of Commerce Dollars for Scholars (Deerfield)
District #205 Endowment Scholarship Fund Dollars for Scholars (Warren)
Dixmoor Educational Foundation Dollars for Scholars
Dixon Rotary Club Dollars for Scholars
Earlville Foundation for Excellence in Education
East Dubuque Business & Tourism Dollars for Scholars
Eisenhower Scholarship Foundation (Blue Island)
Elburn Lions Charities
Elizabeth Lions Club Dollars for Scholars
Elk Grove Village High School Dollars for Scholars
Elmhurst Chamber of Commerce & Industry Dollars for Scholars
Evergreen Park Community High School Scholarship Board
Exchange Club of West DuPage Dollars for Scholars (Wheaton)
F.U.T.U.R.E. Foundation (Ford Heights)
Farmer City Chamber of Commerce Dollars for Scholars
Fisher Community Foundation for Educational Enhancement
Forreston Lions Youth Foundation Dollars for Scholars
Fox River Grove Lions Club Dollars for Scholars

Frankfort Beta Team Dollars for Scholars
G.L.M.V. Chairman's Scholarship Fund Dollars for Scholars (Libertyville)
Galena Lions Dollars for Scholars
Geneseo Chamber of Commerce Dollars for Scholars
Gilman Lions Club Dollars for Scholars
Glendale Heights Chamber of Commerce Dollars for Scholars
Grant Park High School Dollars for Scholars
Grundy County Farm Bureau Foundation (Morris)
Hampshire Lions Dollars for Scholars
Hanover Park Lions Dollars for Scholars
Harlem Scholarship Foundation
Hinsdale/Clarendon Hills Kiwanis Dollars for Scholars
Hoffman Estates Chamber of Commerce Dollars for Scholars
Homer Township Dollars for Scholars
Michael H. Hudson Dollars for Scholars Schol. Fund (Chicago)
Indian Creek Education Foundation (Shabbona)
Joliet Alliance for Youth Dollars for Scholars
Kankakee River Valley Foundation
Kendall County Farm Bureau Foundation (Yorkville)
Kiwanis Club of Bellwood Dollars for Scholars
Kiwanis Club of Bloomington Illinois Charitable Foundation
Kiwanis Club of Brookfield Dollars for Scholars
Kiwanis Club Foundation of Aurora
Kiwanis Club of Normal Dollars for Scholars
Kiwanis Club of Park Forest Dollars for Scholars
Kiwanis Club of Riverside Dollars for Scholars
Kiwanis Club of Woodridge Dollars for Scholars
Lakemoor Dollars for Scholars
Lanark Chamber of Commerce Dollars for Scholars
LaSalle County Farm Bureau Foundation (Ottawa)
Lawndale Service Scholars - Dollars for Scholars (Chicago)
Leland Lions Club Dollars for Scholars Fund
Lena Lions Club Dollars for Scholars
LeRoy Promotion Association/Chamber of Commerce
Lincoln-Way Central New Lenox Dollars for Scholars
Lincoln-Way East Mokena Dollars for Scholars
Lockport Chamber of Commerce Dollars for Scholars
Lombard Chamber of Commerce Dollars for Scholars
MCEP Kiwanis Dollars for Scholars (Elmwood Park)
Maine West Dollars for Scholars (Des Plaines)
Manhattan Chamber of Commerce Dollars for Scholars
Manteno Rotary Club Dollars for Scholars
Maple Park Lions Dollars for Scholars
Markham Educational Foundation Dollars for Scholars
Marseilles Rotary Club Dollars for Scholars
McLean County Farm Bureau Foundation (Bloomington)
Milledgeville Mens Club Dollars for Scholars
Minonk Business Association Dollars for Scholars
Morris Community Initiative for Academic Excellence Dollars for Scholars
Morrison Chamber of Commerce Dollars for Scholars
Mt. Morris Kiwanis Club Dollars for Scholars
Mount Prospect Chamber of Commerce

Dollars for Scholars
Neighborhood Boys & Girls Club (Chicago)
Niles Chamber of Commerce Dollars for Scholars
Oak Park-River Forest Community Foundation
Oregon High School Foundation Dollars for Scholars
Orland Hills Dollars for Scholars
Orland Park Chamber of Commerce Dollars for Scholars
Ottawa Kiwanis Club Dollars for Scholars
Palos Heights Dollars for Scholars
Peotone Community Scholarship Association Inc., Dollars for Scholars
Pontiac Rotary Club Dollars for Scholars
Prairie State College Foundation (Chicago Heights)
Princeton Public Schools Foundation
Prophetstown-Lyndon-Tampico Education Foundation
Prospect Heights Dollars for Scholars
Richards Scholarship Foundation Dollars for Scholars
Ridgeview Education Foundation Dollars for Scholars
Rock Falls Optimist Club Dollars for Scholars
Rockton Lions Club Dollars for Scholars
Rotary Club of Lansing Dollars for Scholars
Rotary Club of Oak Forest Dollars for Scholars
Rotary Club of Romeoville Dollars for Scholars
Sandwich District #430 Foundation for Excellence Dollars for Scholars
Shephard Scholarship Foundation Dollars for Scholars (Palos Heights)
Somonauk Education Foundation Dollars for Scholars
Southwest Youth Collaborative's Dollars for Scholars (Chicago)
Start Smart of Chicago Dollars for Scholars
Stephenson County Farm Bureau Dollars for Scholars
Streamwood Chamber of Commerce Dollars for Scholars
Streator Kiwanis Dollars for Scholars
Stockton Lions Club Dollars for Scholars
Village of Matteson Dollars for Scholars
Village of Monee Dollars for Scholars
Village of Rantoul Dollars for Scholars
Village of Round Lake Beach Dollars for Scholars
Village of Round Lake Heights Dollars for Scholars
Village of Worth Dollars for Scholars Foundation
West Chicago Chamber of Commerce Scholarship Coalition Dollars for Scholars
Westmont Chamber of Commerce Dollars for Scholars
Whiteside County Farm Bureau Foundation (Morrison)
Will County Farm Bureau Foundation (Joliet)
Will County Phi Delta Kappa Dollars for Scholars (Joliet)
Wilmington School District 209-U Foundation for Excellence
Winfield Chamber of Commerce Dollars for Scholars
Woodstock Chamber of Commerce & Industry Dollars for Scholars

INDIANA (98)
Adams Central Scholarship Foundation (Monroe)
Argos Dollars for Scholars
Avon Community Dollars for Scholars (Indianapolis)
Barr-Reeve Scholarship Foundation (Montgomery)
Bellmont Scholarship Foundation (Decatur)

Benton Council for Academic Excellence (Oxford)
CSF of Blackford County (Hartford City)
Blue River Valley Dollars for Scholars (Mt. Summit)
Bluffton/Southern Wells Dollars for Scholars
Borden Dollars for Scholars
Bremen Dollars for Scholars
Brownsburg Educational Foundation, Inc.
Carroll County-Delphi Citizen's Scholarship Foundation
Carver Community Organization Dollars for Scholars (Evansville)
Castle High School Dollars for Scholars (Newburgh)
Caston Community Academic Scholarship Foundation (Fulton)
Center Grove Scholarship Foundation
Community of Attica School. Endowment
Concord Dollars for Scholars (Elkhart)
Corydon Dollars for Scholars
CSF of Covington
Decatur Township Dollars for Scholars (Camby)
Dubois Ruritan Dollars for Scholars
East Chicago Central High School Dollars for Scholars
East Gibson Dollars for Scholars (Oakland City)
East Washington Community Scholarship Foundation (Salem)
Eastbrook Dollars for Scholars (Marion)
Eastern Hancock Dollars for Scholars (Charlottesville)
Ebenezer Baptist Church Dollars for Scholars Foundation (Indianapolis)
CSF of Edinburgh School Community
Elkhart Area Career Center Foundation
Elkhart Central High School Dollars for Scholars
Elkhart Memorial Dollars for Scholars
Fairfield Dollars for Scholars (Goshen)
Franklin Community Dollars for Scholars
Franklin County Dollars for Scholars (Brookville)
Frankton Dollars for Scholars
Fremont Scholarship Foundation
Frontier Dollars for Scholars (Chalmers)
Goshen High School Dollars for Scholars
Hagerstown Community Dollars for Scholars
CSF of Hamilton Hamilton Southeastern Dollars for Scholars Foundation (Fishers)
Hanover Dollars for Scholars (Cedar Lake)
Hauser Community Scholarship Foundation (Hope)
Highland Dollars for Scholars
Hobart River Forest Community School Corporation, Dollars for Scholars
Indian Creek Communities Dollars for Scholars (Morgantown)
Jac-Cen-Del Community Scholarship Foundation (Osgood)
Jefferson Advisory Council Dollars for Scholars (Lafayette)
Kouts High School Memorial ScholarshipFund
Lake Central Dollars for Scholars (St. John)
Lake Station Citizens' Scholarship Foundation
Lakeland Citizens' Scholarship Foundation (LaGrange)
Lanesville Community Dollars for Scholars
Laville CARE Dollars for Scholars (Lakeville)
James C. Lentz Memorial Scholarship Fund, a Dollars for Scholars Chapter (Indianapolis)
Merrillville High School Dollars for Scholars
Milan Scholarship Foundation, Inc.
Mitchell Community Schools Scholarship

Foundation
Morgan Township School Memorial Scholarship Fund (Valparaiso)
Munster Dollars for Scholars
New Castle Dollars for Scholars
North Central High School Dollars for Scholars (Farmersburg)
North Daviess Community Dollars for Scholars (Odon/Plainville)
North Knox Scholarship Foundation (Bicknell)
North Vermillion Dollars for Scholars (Cayuga)
Northern Community Schools Citizens' Scholarship Foundation (Sharpsville)
Northridge Dollars for Scholars (Middlebury)
Northwood Dollars for Scholars (Nappanee)
Norwell Dollars for Scholars (Ossian)
Portage High School Dollars for Scholars
Prairie Heights High School Dollars for Scholars (LaGrange)
Princeton Area Dollars for Scholars
Richmond College Incentive Plan
St. John Missionary Baptist Church, J.W. Bledsoe Scholarship Foundation (Ft. Wayne)
Salem Education Foundation
Shenandoah Dollars for Scholars (Middletown)
Shoals Dollars for Scholars
South Adams Dollars for Scholars (Berne)
South Dearborn Community Scholarship Foundation (Aurora)
South Decatur Area Dollars for Scholars (Greensburg)
South Gibson Dollars for Scholars (Haubstadt)
South Henry Dollars for Scholars (Straughn)
Speedway Citizens' Scholarship Foundation
Springs Valley Dollars for Scholars (French Lick)
Sunman-Dearborn Scholarship Foundation (St. Leon)
Dollars for Scholars of Tell City/Perry
Tipton Scholarship Foundation
Union Community Scholarship Fund (Modoc)
Union Township Scholarship & Education Foundation (Valparaiso)
V.A.L.U.E.S Scholarship Foundation (Hammond)
Valparaiso Scholarship Foundation
Wawasee Dollars for Scholars (Syracuse)
West Central Community Scholarship Fund (Francesville)
Westview Citizens' Scholarship Foundation (Shipshewana)
Whiteland Community High School Dollars for Scholars
Whitko Dollars for Scholars (South Whitley)

IOWA (90)
AGWSR Dollars for Scholars (Ackley)
Algona Community School Foundation
Allamakee Dollars for Scholars (Waukon)
Ames Education Foundation
Anita Dollars for Scholars Foundation
CSF of Ankeny
BC-IG Citizens' Scholarship Foundation (Ida Grove)
CSF of B-G-M (Brooklyn)
Ballard Community Dollars for Scholars (Huxley)
Baxter Community Dollars for Scholars
Belle Plaine School Foundation
Benton Scholarship Foundation
Carlisle Area Dollars for Scholars
Central Community Dollars for Scholars (Elkader)
Charles City Area Dollars for Scholars

Clarinda Foundation, Inc.
Clarke Community Dollars for Scholars (Osceola)
Colfax-Mingo Dollars for Scholars
Creston Dollars for Scholars
Crestwood Dollars for Scholars (Cresco)
Davis County Dollars for Scholars (Bloomfield)
Decorah Community School District Foundation
Denver Dollars for Scholars
Dike-New Hartford Dollars for Scholars
Eagle Grove Area Dollars for Scholars
East Buchanan Citizens' Scholarship Foundation (Winthrop)
East Central Dollars for Scholars (Miles)
East Union Dollars for Scholars Foundation (Afton)
CSF of Eldora-New Providence
English Valleys Citizens' Scholarship Foundation (North English)
CSF of Floyd
Forest City Dollars for Scholars
G-R Dollars for Scholars (Reinbeck)
CSF of Garnavillo
Glenwood Area Dollars for Scholars
Greater Poweshiek Community Foundation (Grinnell)
Griswold Community Dollars for Scholars
Grundy Center Dollars for Scholars
Guttenberg Area Dollars for Scholars
CSF of HLV (Victor)
Hampton-Dumont Dollars for Scholars
I-35 Dollars for Scholars (Truro)
Indianola Area Dollars for Scholars
CSF of Iowa Falls
Janesville Dollars for Scholars
CSF of Jesup
Johnston Dollars for Scholars
L-S Citizens' Scholarship Foundation (Sully)
Lisbon Community School District Foundation
MFL Marmac Dollars for Scholars (Monona)
MMC Educational & Scholarship Foundation (Marcus)
Maquoketa Valley Chapter Dollars for Scholars (Delhi)
CSF of Montezuma Community Schools
Mt. Pleasant Community Dollars for Scholars
New London Dollars for Scholars
CSF of Newton
North Fayette Dollars for Scholars Foundation (West Union)
CSF of Oelwein
CSF of Parkersburg
Pekin Dollars for Scholars
Pella Dollars for Scholars
Postville District Dollars for Scholars
RCL Dollars for Scholars (Rockwell City)
Riceville Community Dollars for Scholars
St. Ansgar Citizens' Scholarship Foundation
Saydel Dollars for Scholars (Des Moines)
Sentral Dollars for Scholars (Fenton)
Solon Dollars for Scholars
South Tama County Scholarship Foundation
South Winneshiek Dollars for Scholars (Calmar)
Southeast Polk Dollars for Scholars Foundation (Runnells)
Southeast Warren Dollars for Scholars (Liberty Center)
Southern Cal School Foundation (Lake City)
Starmont Community Dollars for Scholars (Strawberry Point)
Storm Lake Dollars for Scholars
T-C Dollars for Scholars (Neola)
Tri-County Dollars for Scholars (Thornburg)
Tripoli-Frederika Citizens' Scholarship Foundation
Turkey Valley Foundation Dollars for Scholars (Jackson Junction)

CSF of Twin Cedars Community Schools (Bussey)
Union Community Dollars for Scholars (LaPorte City)
CSF of Urbandale
Valley Community Dollars for Scholars (Elgin)
CSF of Vinton
Waterloo Community Dollars for Scholars
Waukee Community School Foundation
Waverly-Shell Rock Dollars for Scholars Presidential Foundation
West Central Community Dollars for Scholars (Stuart)
West Des Moines Community Schools Foundation for Educational Excellence
Woden-Crystal Lake-Titonka Dollars for Scholars Scholarship Foundation

KANSAS (1)
CSF of Phillips County (Phillipsburg)

KENTUCKY (2)
Lincoln County Educational Fund, Inc. (Stanford)
Dollars for Scholars of Owensboro-Daviess County

LOUISIANA (2)
Dollars for Scholars Jefferson
New Orleans Public School Scholarship Foundation

MAINE (21)
Boothbay Region Student Aid Fund, Inc.
Border Trust Dollars for Scholars (South China)
Brunswick Area Student Aid Fund
Calais Dollars for Scholars
Greater Portland Dollars for Scholars
CSF of Hampden-Newburgh-Winterport
The Island Institute (Rockland)
The Maine Sea Coast Missionary Society (Bar Harbor)
A. Cressy Morrison Dollars for Scholars (Deer Isle)
Morse High School Scholarship Fund (Bath)
Norway-Paris Kiwanis Charitable Foundation
CSF of Sacopee Valley (South Hiram)
CSF of SAD 29 - Houlton
CSF of SAD 54 – Skowhegan
Shead High School Dollars for Scholars (Eastport)
CSF of South Aroostook Community Scholarship District (Island Falls)
UMaine Upward Bound Dollars for Scholars (Orono)
Van Buren Dollars for Scholars
Wells High School Scholarship Foundation Dollars for Scholars
CSF of Yarmouth
York Mentor Scholarship Fund-Dollars for Scholars

MARYLAND (7)
Donnell E. Bacon Memorial Scholarship Fund (Baltimore)
The Centreville Rotary Club's Dollars for Scholars
Easton Rotary Dollars for Scholars
Park Heights Scholarship Fund (Baltimore)
CSF of St. Mary's County (Leonardtown)
Scholarships for Scholars (Annapolis)
Seat Pleasant Dollars for Scholars

MASSACHUSETTS (76)
CSF of Abington
Alumni & Friends of Lynn Classical High School, Inc.
Andover Dollars for Scholars
Arlington Citizens Scholarship Foundation
CSF of Bedford
Belmont Scholarship Fund
Berkshire Taconic Community Foundation (Great Barrington)

Beverly Dollars for Scholars
The Boston Foundation
The Boxford Public Library and Perley Scholarship Funds
CSF of Bridgewater-Raynham
Bristol Community College Upward Bound Dollars for Scholars (Fall River)
Brockton Dollars for Scholars
Burlington Community Scholarship Foundation, Inc.
Joseph Case High School Scholarship Trust Funds, Inc. (Swansea)
CSF of Chatham
Community Foundation of Cape Cod (Yarmouthport)
Community Foundation of Western Massachusetts (Springfield)
Concord-Carlisle Scholarship Fund
CSF of Dighton-Rehoboth
Dracut Scholarship Foundation
Peter Medoff Dudley Youth Scholarship Fund (Boston)
East Cambridge Scholarship Fund
CSF of Easthampton
CSF of Fall River
Donald A. Fisher Citizens' Scholarship Foundation (West Bridgewater)
Gloucester Scholarship Foundation
CSF of Granville-Tolland
Hancock Community Dollars for Scholars
CSF of Harwich
CSF of Holliston
CSF of Lanesboro
Latino Scholarship Association (Holyoke)
Lincoln-Sudbury Scholarship Fund, Inc.
Lynnfield Scholarship Foundation, Inc.
METCO College Scholarship Fund of Lexington
CSF of Mansfield
CSF of Marblehead, Inc.
CSF of Marlborough, Inc.
Methuen Scholarship Foundation
CSF of Middleboro
CSF of Millbury
CSF of Millis
Minnechaug Scholarship Foundation (Wilbraham)
Nashoba Regional Scholarship Foundation (Bolton)
Newton Dollars for Scholars
North Adams Dollars for Scholars
North Andover Scholarship Foundation, Inc.
North Reading Dollars for Scholars, Citizens' Scholarship Foundation
CSF of Northampton
Northborough Scholarship Advisory Committee
Norwood Scholarship Foundation, Inc.
CSF of Pittsfield
Reading Scholarship Foundation, Inc.
CSF of Rockland
CSF of Sherborn
CSF of Somerset
City of Somerville Dollars for Scholars
Somerville High School Scholarship Foundation
Somerville Mathematics Dollars for Scholars Fund
Southborough Scholarship Advisory Committee
CSF of Southwick
Town of Billerica Scholarship Foundation
The Town of Dedham Scholarship Committee
Town of Weymouth Scholarship Fund
CSF of Uxbridge
CSF of Wakefield
City of Waltham Scholarship Fund
Wayland High School Scholarship Committee
Wellesley Hills Junior Woman's Club
Wellesley Scholarship Foundation, Inc.
West Boylston Scholarship Foundation
CSF of Westfield, Inc.
CSF of Whitman-Hanson
Woburn High School Scholarship Fund, Inc

Worcester Latino Dollars for Scholars

MICHIGAN (2)
CSF of Allegan
Willow Run/Ypsilanti Dollars for Scholars

MINNESOTA (129)
Aitkin Area Dollars for Scholars
CSF of Alexandria
Ashby Area Dollars for Scholars
Barnesville Dollars for Scholars
Barnum Citizens' Scholarship Foundation
Becker Dollars for Scholars
CSF of Belle Plaine
Bertha-Hewitt Dollars for Scholars
CSF of Blackduck
CSF of Blooming Prairie
Blue Earth Educational Assistance, Inc.
CSF of Braham
CSF of Brandon
CSF of Breckenridge
CSF of Browerville
The Larry Brown Youth Education Corporation (Minneapolis)
Cambridge-Isanti Dollars for Scholars Foundation
Cedar Mountain Dollars for Scholars (Morgan)
Chisago Lakes Education Foundation (Lindstrom)
CSF of Cleveland
Climax-Shelly Dollars for Scholars
Cloquet Community Scholarship Fund
Comfrey Area Dollars for Scholars
CSF of Cromwell-Wright
CSF of Dassel-Cokato
Delano Area Dollars for Scholars
Detroit Lakes Scholarship Foundation
CSF of Dilworth-Glyndon-Felton
District 883 Dollars for Scholars (Rockford)
Eagan Foundation, The
Eagle Valley Dollars for Scholars (Clarissa)
East Central Dollars for Scholars (Sandstone)
Eastview Community Foundation (Apple Valley)
Esko Educational Foundation
CSF of Evansville
CSF of Fairmont School District 454
Faribault Area Public School Education Trust Association
Fergus Falls Area Dollars for Scholars
Fillmore Central Dollars for Scholars (Harmony)
Floodwood Dollars for Scholars
G-F-W Dollars for Scholars (Winthrop)
Garrison Dollars for Scholars
Glenville-Emmons Dollars for Scholars
Granada-Huntley-East Chain Dollars for Scholars
CSF of Granite Falls
Hawley Dollars for Scholars
Henning Student Aid Foundation
Herman/Norcross Dollars for Scholars
Hutchinson Area Dollars for Scholars
Jackson County Central Dollars for Scholars
CSF of the Jasper School Area
Earl C. Joseph Future Thought Leadership Dollars for Scholars (St. Paul)
CSF of Kasson-Mantorville
Kimball Area Dollars for Scholars
LCWM Dollars for Scholars (Lake Crystal)
Lac qui Parle Valley Dollars for Scholars (Madison)
CSF of Lake Benton
CSF of Lake of the Woods
Lake Park Dollars for Scholars
LeRoy-Ostrander Dollars for Scholars
LeSueur-Henderson Dollars for Scholars
Pam Lindow Foundation of Nevis
CSF of Long Prairie
CSF of Luverne
MTCMB/Project Cope (St. Paul)
Mankato/North Mankato Area Dollars for Scholars
Maple River Dollars for Scholars (Mapleton)

Martin County West Dollars for Scholars (Welcome)
McLeod County East Dollars for Scholars (Lester Prairie)
Menahga Dollars for Scholars Foundation
Milaca Scholarship Foundation
Minneota Dollars for Scholars
Minnewaska Area Dollars for Scholars (Glenwood)
Moorhead Foundation Dollars for Scholars
CSF of Moose Lake
Mora Dollars for Scholars
Morris Area School District No. 769 Foundation
Morrison County Student Loan Association, Inc. (Little Falls)
Morristown Dollars for Scholars
Mountain Lake Dollars for Scholars
Neighborhood House (St. Paul)
New Prague Dollars for Scholars
Norman County West Dollars for Scholars (Halstad)
Northland Scholarship Fund, Inc. (Remer)
Norwood Young America Dollars for Scholars
CSF of Ogilvie
CSF of Osakis
Parkers Prairie School District 547
CSF of Paynesville
Dollars for Scholars, People's View Enterprises (Minneapolis)
Perham Citizens' Scholarship Foundation
Ricky Peterson Memorial Scholarship Foundation (Houston)
Pine River-Backus Dollars for Scholars
CSF of Pipestone School District 583
Pride In the Tiger Foundation (Marshall)
Princeton Scholarship Foundation
Prior Lake Women of Today
RTR Dollars for Scholars (Tyler)
CSF of Randolph
Redwood Area Dollars for Scholars Orrin S. Estebo Chapter
Rocori Area Dollars for Scholars (Cold Spring)
CSF of Rush City
St. Joseph Area Dollars for Scholars
St. Louis Park Dollars for Scholars
St. Paul Friend of Youth Foundation
CSF of St. Peter-Kasota
CSF of Sauk Centre
Scholarship Fund of Madelia School District 837
School District #4 Foundation (McGregor)
School District 110 Foundation (Waconia)
CSF of Sebeka
Shakopee Dollars for Scholars
CSF of Sleepy Eye
Spring Grove Dollars for Scholars
Staples & Motley Dollars for Scholars
Swanville Community Scholarship Fund, Inc.
Tracy Area Dollars for Scholars
Twin Cities Business, Engineering, Science & Technology (BEST) Dollars for Scholars (Plymouth)
Twin Valley Dollars for Scholars
Upsula Area Dollars for Scholars
CSF of Verndale
CSF of Wabasha-Kellogg
Wadena-Deer Creek Dollars for Scholars
Waubun-Ogema-White Earth Dollars for Scholars
West Central Area Dollars for Scholars (Elbow Lake)
Westbrook-Walnut Grove Dollars for Scholars
CSF of Wheaton
CSF of Windom
CSF of Worthington

MONTANA (7)
Bainville Dollars for Scholars Foundation
Brady Dollars for Scholars
Conrad Dollars for Scholars

Custer County Education Foundation (Miles City)
Polson Dollars for Scholars
Red Lodge Area Dollars for Scholars Foundation
Sidney Area Dollars for Scholars

NEBRASKA (40)
Ainsworth High School Dollars for Scholars Activity Scholarship
Banner County Dollars for Scholars (Harrisburg)
Blue Hill Dollars for Scholars
Burwell Dollars for Scholars
Coleridge Community Education Foundation Dollars for Scholars
Denton Dollars for Scholars
Elgin Dollars for Scholars
Fairbury Public Schools Foundation
Friends of Oakland Dollars for Scholars
Garden County Turner Youth Dollars for Scholars (Oshkosh)
Gordon Dollars for Scholars
Grant Public Schools Foundation
CSF of the Heartland (Omaha)
Johnson-Brock Dollars for Scholars
Johnson County Dollars for Scholars (Tecumseh)
Loup County Scholarship Fund Dollars for Scholars (Taylor)
Lyons Community Foundation
Mead Educational Foundation
Morrill Schools Foundation
Nebraska Teacher World Dollars for Scholars (Wayne)
Palisade Community Foundation Dollars for Scholars
Phelps County Community Foundation (Holdrege)
Plattsmouth Community Foundation's Dollars for Scholars
Potter-Dix Dollars for Scholars
Red Cloud Community Foundation/Red Cloud Community Schools Dollars for Scholars
SEM Dollars for Scholars (Sumner)
St. Cecilia's High School Endowment Fund
Shelby Dollars for Scholars
Spencer Dollars for Scholars Program
Sutton Educational Foundation Dollars for Scholars
Syracuse Foundation Inc., Dollars for Scholars
TeamMates of Franklin County (Franklin)
Valentine Turner Foundation Dollars for Scholars
Valley County Dollars for Scholars (Ord)
Wallace Community Foundation
Wayne Public Schools Foundation
West Central Sandhills Education Foundation Dollars for Scholars (Hyannis)
West Holt High School Foundation Dollars for Scholars (Atkinson)
Wilcox Area Community Foundation Dollars for Scholars
Wood River Dollars for Scholars

NEVADA (1)
Virgin Valley Dollars for Scholars (Mesquite)

NEW HAMPSHIRE (20)
CSF of Auburn
The Justin Brabant Memorial Dollars for Scholars Foundation (Derry)
Candia Dollars for Scholars
CSF of Con-Val School District (Petersborough)
CSF of Fall Mountain Regional School District (Langdon)
CSF of Farmington
CSF of Franklin, Inc.
CSF of Gorham-Randolph-Shelburne
Greater Pittsfield Citizens' Scholarship Foundation, Inc.
CSF of Hollis/Brookline
Lakes Region Scholarship Foundation (Gilford)

CSF of Lebanon
CSF of Londonderry
CSF of Mascoma Valley (Enfield)
The Jeff Morin Memorial Scholarship Fund (Nashua)
Dollars for Scholars of Mount Washington Valley (North Conway)
New Hampshire Charitable Foundation (Concord)
CSF of Salem
CSF of Souhegan Valley (Millford)
Winnacunnet High Scholarship Foundation, Inc. (Exeter)

NEW JERSEY (11)
CSF of Atlantic City (Ventnor City)
Burlington Township Schools Scholarship Committee
Citizens' Scholarship Committee of Pitman, Inc.
Clearview Community Scholarship Committee (Mullica Hill)
Lawrence High School Dollars for Scholars (Lawrenceville)
CSF of Mahwah
Dollars for Scholars of Northern New Jersey
Pennsauken High School Foundation
Princeton Regional Scholarship Foundation
The Don Smith Memorial Scholarship Fund (Port Republic)
South Plainfield Vision 2001 Education Foundation, Inc.

NEW YORK (107)
ACORNS-Alexander Community Organization for Renewable and New Scholarships (East Aurora)
Alden Community Scholarship Foundation "Dollars for Scholars"
CSF of Altmar-Parish-Williamstown
CSF of Andes School Support Organization
Argyle Community Scholarship Committee
Baldwinsville Community Scholarship Foundation, Inc.
Belleville-Henderson Dollars for Scholars
Belmont Rotary Dollars for Scholars
Binghamton Dollars for Scholars
Brothertown Scholarship Fund (Waterville)
Cairo-Durham Dollars for Scholars
Canaseraga Citizens' Scholarship Foundation
CSF of Canastota School District
Center for Urban Education/Dollars for Scholars (New York City)
Charlotte Valley Central School Dollars for Scholars (Davenport)
Chenango Forks Scholarship Foundation
CSF of Chittenango Central School
CSF of Clinton
Clyde-Savannah Dollars for Scholars
Colesville Dollars for Scholars (Harpursville)
Colton-Pierrepont Dollars for Scholars Community Scholarship Foundation
Dollars for Scholars of Commack
Corinth Dollars for Scholars Foundation
CSF of Corona-East Elmhurst
Deposit Education Endowment Program, Inc.
DeRuyter Dollars for Scholars
Dollars for Schuylkill Scholars (Pottsville)
Dollars for Scholars of Dover UFSD (Dover Plains)
Dundee Dollars for Scholars
East Greenbush Education Foundation
Fairport-Perinton Dollars for Scholars
Freeport Dollars for Scholars
Friends of Broome-Tioga BOCES/Dollars for Scholars
Gananda Dollars for Scholars (Walworth)
Geneva High School Dollars for Scholars
CSF of Gilboa
Greene Dollars for Scholars

Greenville Central School District
Dollars for Scholars
The Hancock Community Education Foundation
Hannibal Dollars for Scholars
Herkimer BOCES Dollars for Scholars
CSF of Island Trees (Levittown)
Johnsburg Dollars for Scholars (North Creek)
Johnson City Dollars for Scholars
CSF of Jordan-Elbridge
Leuze-Reardon-Belloff Scholarship Committee (Adams)
Levittown Public Schools Dollars for Scholars
The Liberty Partnership Program at the Center for Women in Government & Civil Society Dollars for Scholars
Chapter (Albany)
CSF of Liverpool
Maine Endwell Dollars for Scholars Scholarship Foundation
CSF of Margaretville Central School
Marion Dollars for Scholars
Dollars for Scholars of Medina
CSF of Mexico, New Haven, Palermo
Minerva Chapter of Dollars for Scholars (Olmsteadville)
The Nanuet Rotary Scholarship Foundation, Inc.
The New Lebanon Foundation/Dollars for Scholars
North Rose-Wolcott Community Dollars for Scholars
CSF of North Syracuse Central School
Dist.
North Warren Dollars for Scholars (Chestertown)
Northern New York Community Foundation Dollars for Scholars (Watertown)
Nyack Rotary Scholarship Fund
Oakfield-Alabama Dollars for Scholars
Oneonta Dollars for Scholars
Onondaga Central Schools Education Foundation Board (Nedrow)
Ontario/Walworth Dollars for Scholars
Owego Apalachin Dollars for Scholars
Oxford Academy and Central School District Dollars for Scholars
Palmyra-Macedon Central School Dist.
Penfield Scholarship Association
Penn Yan Dollars for Scholars
CSF of Phoenix School District
CSF of Port Byron School District
Portville Community Dollars for
Scholars
Putnam Founders Dollars for Scholars
Queensbury Dollars for Scholars
Red Jacket Scholarship Committee (Shortsville)
CSF of Rhinebeck
CSF of Rome
CSF of Roxbury
SUNY Plattsburgh Upward Bound Dollars for Scholars
CSF of Sandy Creek Central School
District
Schalmont Dollars for Scholars
(Rotterdam)
Scholarship Association of Lake George
Schuylerville Dollars for Scholars
CSF of Seaford
Shenendehowa Dollars for Scholars (Clifton Park)
CSF of Sidney
South Kortright Citizens' Scholarship Foundation
Southern Cayuga Scholarship
Foundation (Aurora)
CSF of Stamford
Susquehanna Valley Dollars for
Scholars (Conklin)
Sweet Home Central School District (Tonawanda)
Syracuse Liberty Partnerships Dollars
for Scholars
Dollars for Scholars of Taconic Hills (Hillsdale)
Unadilla Valley Dollars for Scholars
Unatego Dollars for Scholars (Otego)
Union-Endicott Dollars for Scholars Foundation
Utica Dollars for Scholars

CSF of Vernon-Verona-Sherrill
Vestal Dollars for Scholars
Victor Scholarship Program
Voorheesville Dollars for Scholars
Walton Dollars for Scholars
CSF of Wantagh
Warrensburg Scholarship Association, Inc.
Williamson Dollars for Scholars
Windsor/Kirkwood Dollars for Scholars

NORTH DAKOTA (62)
Aneta, Kloten, McVille, Pekin, Tolna Area Dollars for Scholars
Beach, Golva, Medora & Sentinel Butte Area Dollars for Scholars
Belfield Area Dollars for Scholars
Beulah Area Dollars for Scholars
Bowman Area Dollars for Scholars
Buffalo, Fingal, Tower City Area Dollars for Scholars
Carrington Area Dollars for Scholars
Cavalier Area Dollars for Scholars
Center Area Dollars for Scholars
Central Cass Dollars for Scholars (Casselton)
Dickinson Area Dollars for Scholars
Divide County Area Dollars for Scholars (Crosby)
Edgeley Dollars for Scholars
Elgin/New Leipzig Area Dollars for Scholars
Ellendale Area Dollars for Scholars
Enderlin Area Dollars for Scholars
Fargo Area Dollars for Scholars
Garrison Dollars for Scholars
Glen Ullin Area Dollars for Scholars
Glenburn Area Dollars for Scholars Foundation
CSF of Grand Forks-East Grand Forks
Halliday Area Dollars for Scholars
Hankinson Dollars for Scholars
Hatton Area Dollars for Scholars
Hazelton-Moffit-Braddock Area Dollars for Scholars
Hazen Area Dollars for Scholars
Hebron Area Dollars for Scholars
Hillsboro Scholarship Foundation
Jamestown Public School Foundation
Kidder County Area Dollars for Scholars (Steele)
Killdeer Area Dollars for Scholars
Kindred Area Dollars for Scholars
Kulm Area Dollars for Scholars
LHS Club/Dollars for Scholars (LaMoure)
Lakota Michigan Unity Area Dollars for Scholars
Lisbon Dollars for Scholars
Litchville-Marion Dollars for Scholars
Mayville Portland Clifford Galesburg Area Dollars for Scholars
Milnor Area Dollars for Scholars
Minot Area Dollars for Scholars
Mott Area Dollars for Scholars
Napoleon Dollars for Scholars
New Salem-Almont Area Dollars for Scholars
New Town Area Dollars for Scholars
North Central Area Dollars for Scholars
Northern Cass Dollars for Scholars (Hunter)
Northwood Area Dollars for Scholars
Page Area Dollars for Scholars
Regent Area Dollars for Scholars
Rugby Dollars for Scholars
Sheridan County Dollars for Scholars (Goodrich)
TEEF/Dollars for Scholars (Thompson)
Tioga Area Dollars for Scholars
Turtle Lake-Mercer Dollars for Scholars
Velva Area Dollars for Scholars
Wahpeton Dollars for Scholars
Washburn Area Dollars for Scholars
Watford City Area Dollars for Scholars
West Fargo Dollars for Scholars
Wilton Area Dollars for Scholars
Wishek Area Dollars for Scholars
Wyndmere Area Dollars for Scholars

OHIO (15)

CSF of Bath Local School District (Lima)
CSF of Coshocton County
CSF of Delaware County
CSF of East Clinton (New Vienna)
CSF of Greenville
CSF of Guernsey County (Cambridge)
Lake Academic Booster Club (Uniontown)
CSF of Medina
CSF of Newcomerstown
CSF of Norwalk
CSF of Springfield/Holland
Tri-State Area Citizens' Scholarship Foundation (East Liverpool)
CSF of Troy
CSF of Wapakoneta
Withrow Dollars for Scholars

OREGON (8)
Bobcat Foundation/Dollars for Scholars (Union)
Condon Dollars for Scholars Foundation
Days Creek Dollars for Scholars Foundation
Gaston Dollars for Scholars Foundation
Harney County Dollars for Scholars (Burns)
Harrisburg Dollars for Scholars Foundation
South Morrow County Scholarship Trust (Heppner)
South Umpqua Valley Dollars for Scholars (Myrtle Creek)

PENNSYLVANIA (19)
Beaver-Leeds Dollars for Scholars (Philadelphia)
Bedford Area Dollars for Scholars
Berks County Community Foundation, Inc. (Reading)
Central York Dollars for Scholars (York)
Community Scholarship Foundation of Canon-McMillan (Cannonsburg)
Conewago Valley Dollars for Scholars Foundation
Dallastown Area Dollars for Scholars
Eastern York Dollars for Scholars (Wrightsville)
CSF of Lancaster County
Northeastern School District Scholarship Foundation (Manchester)
Red Lion Area Educational Foundation
South Eastern Dollars for Scholars (Fawn Grove)
South Western Dollars for Scholars (Hanover)
Southern York County School District Foundation (Glen Rock)
Spring Grove Area Scholarship Foundation
West York Area Dollars for Scholars (York)
York City Dollars for Scholars
York Suburban Dollars for Scholars

RHODE ISLAND (11)
CSF of Barrington
Chamber Education Foundation (Warwick)
Community 2000 Education Foundation (Charlestown)
Community College of Rhode Island Foundation (Warwick)
CSF of East Providence
Latino Dollars for Scholars of Rhode Island Foundation (Greater Providence)
CSF of Little Compton
CSF of North Providence
CSF of Portsmouth
Rhode Island College Upward Bound Dollars for Scholars (Providence)
CSF of Scituate

SOUTH CAROLINA (3)
Aiken County Dollars for Scholars
Laurens County Education Enrichment Fund
CSF of North Charleston

SOUTH DAKOTA (1)

Arlington Dollars for Scholars

TEXAS (2)
El Campo Academic Booster Club
Wharton Academic Booster Club

VERMONT (12)
CSF of Bennington
Brattleboro Sunrise Rotary Dollars for Scholars
Gateway Foundation, Inc. (Brattleboro)
Leland & Gray Educational Foundation, Inc. (Newfane)
Elsie Litwhiler Dollars for Scholars (Johnson)
Mill River Union High School Dollars for Scholars (North Clarendon)
Spaulding High School Dollars for Scholars (Barre)
Town of Canaan Dollars for Scholars
Twinfield Scholarship Committee (Plainfield)
UVM Upward Bound Dollars for Scholars (Burlington)
Upward Bound Dollars for Scholars (Lyndonville)
Winooski Dollars for Scholars Foundation

VIRGINIA (1)
CSF of Shenandoah County (Woodstock)

WASHINGTON (109)
Adna Scholarship Foundation
African American Dollars for Scholars Foundation (Seattle)
Almira, Coulee, Hartline Dollars for Scholars
Arlington Dollars for Scholars
Auburn Optimist Dollars for Scholars Foundation
Battle Ground Dollars for Scholars
Bellingham Dollars for Scholars
Bethel Educational Scholarship Team (Spanaway)
Blaine Scholarship Foundation
Boistfort Lions Dollars for Scholars (Curtis)
Brewster Kiwanis Dollars for Scholars
Bridgeport Dollars for Scholars Foundation
Burlington Edison School District Foundation
Centralia High School Dollars for Scholars Foundation
Chehalis Dollars for Scholars
Cheney Area Dollars for Scholars
Chewelah Scholarship Foundation
Colville Dollars for Scholars Foundation
Cosmopolis Dollars for Scholars Foundation
Curtis Vikings Dollars for Scholars (University Place)
Cusick Dollars for Scholars Foundation
Deer Park Dollars for Scholars
Des Moines Dollars for Scholars
East Valley Dollars for Scholars (Yakima)
Eatonville Dollars for Scholars Foundation
Edmonds School District #15 Alumni Association (Lynnwood)
Entiat Dollars for Scholars Foundation
Evergreen High School Dollars for Scholars (Vancouver)
Evergreen Scholarship Foundation
Ferndale Dollars for Scholars
Fidalgo Island Educational Youth Foundation (Anacortes)
Fife High School Scholarship Foundation
Friends of Sealth Dollars for Scholars Foundation (Seattle)
Garfield Dollars for Scholars Foundation
Grandview Dollars for Scholars Foundation
Harrington Dollars for Scholars
Heritage High School Chapter of Dollars for Scholars (Vancouver)
Hidden Heritage Dollars for Scholars

(Auburn)
Joyce Community Scholarship Foundation
Kettle Falls School District Scholarship Program
LETI Dollars for Scholars (Lynnwood)
La Center Community Scholarship Foundation
La Conner Community Scholarship Foundation
La Crosse Dollars for Scholars
Lopez Island Dollars for Scholars Foundation
Lynden Dollars for Scholars Foundation
Mabton Dollars for Scholars
McCleary Scholarship Fund
Mansfield Dollars for Scholars
John Marshall High School Dollars for Scholars Foundation (Seattle)
Medical Lake Dollars for Scholars
Mercer Island Dollars for Scholars
Meridian Public Schools Foundation (Bellingham)
Methow Valley Dollars for Scholars Foundation (Twisp)
Mount Baker Scholarship Foundation (Deming)
Mount Vernon Chamber Dollars for Scholars Foundation
Naches Dollars for Scholars
Nooksack Valley Dollars for Scholars Foundation
North Mason Dollars for Scholars (Belfair)
North River Dollars for Scholars Foundation (Cosmopolis)
Northport Dollars for Scholars
Orondo Dollars for Scholars Foundation
Oroville Dollars for Scholars Foundation
Orting Alumni Schol. Foundation
P.A.A.S.E. at Garfield High School Dollars for Scholars (Seattle)
P.A.E.F. Alumni Association/Dollars for Scholars (Port Angeles)
Pateros School Dollars for Scholars Foundation
Pe Ell Trojan Booster Club Dollars for Scholars
Peninsula Hawks Scholarship Fund (Gig Harbor)
Point Roberts Dollars for Scholars
Pomeroy Dollars for Scholars
Port Townsend High School Scholarship Foundation
Puyallup Schools Foundation
Quilcene-Brinnon Dollars for Scholars
Rainier Beach High School Dollars for Scholars
Riverside Dollars for Scholars
Bernadette Roozen-Miller Memorial Dollars for Scholars Foundation (Mt. Vernon)
Rosalia Dollars for Scholars
St. John-Endicott Cooperative Schools Foundation Dollars for Scholars Program
San Juan Island Dollars for Scholars Foundation (Friday Harbor)
Satsop Dollars for Scholars Foundation
Selkirk Dollars for Scholars (Ione)
Sequim Dollars for Scholars
Shoreline Chamber of Commerce Dollars for Scholars
Snohomish County Community Foundation (Everett)
South Bend Kiwanis Club, Inc.
South Whidbey Schools Foundation (South Whidbey Island)
Spokane Indian Dollars for Scholars (Wellpinit)
Stanwood Camano Area Foundation
Steilacoom Historical Education Foundation
Sumner-Bonney Lake Dollars for Scholars
Sunnyside Dollars for Scholars
Tenino Dollars for Scholars Foundation
Toppenish-Wapato Dollars for Scholars
Treehouse Fund (Seattle)
Tyee High School Dollars for Scholars Foundation
United Snoqualmie Valley Scholarship Foundation

Vashon Community Scholarship Foundation
Wahkiakum Dollars for Scholars (Cathlamet)
Mary Walker Community Dollars for Scholars (Springdale)
Warden Dollars for Scholars
Washington State Retired Teachers Foundation (Olympia)
Washtucna-Benge Dollars for Scholars
West Valley Dollars for Scholars Foundation (Yakima)
White River Dollars for Scholars (Buckley)
Wilson Creek Dollars for Scholars Foundation
Winlock Dollars for Scholars

Yakima Hispanic Academic Achievers Program
Yelm Dollars for Scholars

WEST VIRGINIA (4)
CSF of Beckley
CSF of New Martinsville
CSF of Shady Spring District
CSF of Trap Hill-Liberty

WISCONSIN (21)
Bangor Scholarship Foundation
Beaver Dam Scholarship Foundation, Inc.
Bowler Alumni Dollars for Scholars
Cashton High School Scholarship Foundation
Clayton Community Dollars for Scholars
CSF of Clear Lake
Ellsworth Area Dollars for Scholars
CSF of Florence County
CSF of Frederic
Grantsburg Community Scholarship Foundation
Gresham Dollars for Scholars
Highland Area Dollars for Scholars
Menomonie Area Public Schools Foundation, Inc.
Niagara Area Citizens' Scholarship Foundation
Oconto Falls Dollars for Scholars
Princeton Wisconsin Dollars for Scholars
St. Croix Falls District Scholarship Foundation
Sauk Prairie Foundation for Academic Excellence (Prairie du Sac)
Shawano Dollars for Scholars
Somerset Memorial Scholarship Fund, Inc.
Unity Educational Scholarship Foundation, Inc. (Balsam Lake)

1,117 Total Chapters
38 States Plus Washington, D.C.

8/28/02
h:\documents\dif\monthend\ds-list.doc

APPENDIX D

CSFA Collegiate Partners (as of July, 2002)

COLLEGIATE PARTNERS

A program of Citizens' Scholarship Foundation of America, Inc.

CALIFORNIA (34/14)
Azusa Pacific University
California Baptist University*
California Institute of the Arts*
California State Polytechnic University - Pomona†
California State University-Dominguez Hills*
California State University, Hayward†
California State University-Long Beach
California State University-Northridge*†
California State University-San Bernardino
California State University-San Marcos†
Chapman University
Concordia University*
La Sierra University*
Loyola Marymount University
Marymount College*
Mount St. Mary's College*
Occidental College*†
Pepperdine University
Point Loma Nazarene College
Rancho Santiago Community College District
Riverside Community College*
San Diego State University
Santa Clara University
Sonoma State University
University of California-Irvine†
University of California-Los Angeles*
University of California-Riverside*†
University of California-San Diego
University of La Verne
University of the Pacific
University of San Diego†
University of Southern California*
Westmont College*
Whittier College

CONNECTICUT (8/2)
Albertus Magnus College
Connecticut College
Fairfield University*
Sacred Heart University*
Saint Joseph College
University of Connecticut
Wesleyan University†
Yale University†

DELAWARE (1)
University of Delaware

DISTRICT OF COLUMBIA (1)
(The) George Washington University

FLORIDA (7/4)
Eckerd College*†
Florida Atlantic University*
Florida Southern College
Nova Southeastern University
Palm Beach Atlantic College
Palm Beach Community College*
University of Miami*†

GEORGIA (1)
Brenau University

HAWAII (1)
Hawaii Pacific University

IDAHO (1/1)
Idaho State University*

ILLINOIS (19/4)
Augustana College
Aurora University
Blackburn College
Bradley University†
Columbia College
Elmhurst College*†
Greenville College*
Illinois Wesleyan University
Judson College
Kendall College
Knox College
Lewis University
MacCormac College*
Millikin University
North Central College
Northwestern University
Trinity Christian College*
University of St. Francis
Wheaton College†

INDIANA (26/8)
Ancilla College
Ball State University†
Butler University
DePauw University†
Earlham College
Franklin College*
Goshen College
Grace College
Hanover College
Huntington College*
Indiana Institute of Technology*
Indiana University Northwest†
Indiana University Purdue University-Indianapolis
Indiana Wesleyan University*†
Manchester College*
Marian College*
Oakland City University*
Rose-Hulman Institute of Technology
Saint Mary's College†
Taylor University*†
University of Evansville
University of Indianapolis†
University of Notre Dame
University of St. Francis
Valparaiso University
Vincennes University

IOWA (34/16)
American Institute of Business*
Buena Vista University*
Capri College
Central College†
Clarke College†
Coe College*†
Cornell College*
Des Moines Area Community College
Des Moines University - Osteopathic Medical Center
Dordt College
Drake University*†
Grand View College*
Grinnell College*
Hawkeye Community College
Iowa State University
Iowa Wesleyan College
Kirkwood Community College
Loras College*†
Luther College
Mount Mercy College
Northeast Iowa Community College*
North Iowa Area Community College*
Northwestern College
Northwest Iowa Community College*
Simpson College†
Southeastern Community College*
Southwestern Community College (Creston)*
University of Dubuque*†
University of Iowa†
University of Northern Iowa
Upper Iowa University*
Waldorf College*
Wartburg College†
William Penn University

KENTUCKY (7/2)
Bellarmine College*
Cumberland College*
Kentucky Wesleyan College
Pikeville College
Thomas More College
Transylvania University

Thomas More College
Transylvania University
University of Kentucky

LOUISIANA (1)
Dillard University

MAINE (10/1)
Bates College
Bowdoin College†
Colby College
Maine College of Art
Maine Maritime Academy†
Saint Joseph's College*
University of Maine at Farmington†
University of Maine-Orono
University of Southern Maine
Washington County Technical College

MARYLAND (3)
Goucher College
Johns Hopkins University†
University of Maryland at College Park

MASSACHUSETTS (47/9)
Amherst College
Assumption College*
Babson College
Bentley College
Boston College†
Boston University†
Brandeis University
Bristol Community College*
Clark University
College of the Holy Cross†
Emerson College
Emmanuel College
Endicott College*†
Franklin Institute of Boston
Gordon College
Hampshire College*
Harvard University †
Lasell College
Lesley College*
Marian Court College
Massachusetts College of Art
Massachusetts College of Liberal Arts
Merrimack College
Montserrat College of Art
Mount Holyoke College
Newbury College
New England Conservatory of Music
Nichols College*
Northeastern University†
Regis College
Salem State College
Simmons College
Smith College
Stonehill College*†
Suffolk University*
Tufts University†
University of Massachusetts Amherst
University of Massachusetts Boston†
University of Massachusetts Dartmouth†
University of Massachusetts Lowell
Wentworth Institute of Technology*
Westfield State College
Wheaton College†
Wheelock College
Williams College†
Worcester Polytechnic Institute
Worcester State College†

MICHIGAN (4/1)
Adrian College*
Albion College
Calvin College†
University of Michigan-Dearborn†

MINNESOTA (42/10)
Alexandria Technical College*
Art Institute International Minnesota
Augsburg College†
Bethany Lutheran College
Bethel College†
Carleton College†
Century Community and Technical College
College of St. Benedict†
College of St. Catherine†
College of St. Scholastica*
Concordia College-Moorhead
Crown College†
Dunwoody Institute*

Globe College, Inc.
Gustavus Adolphus College
Hamline University
Macalester College
(The) McConnell School, Inc.
Medical Institute of Minnesota
Metropolitan State University
The Minneapolis College of Art and Design*
Minnesota School of Business
Minnesota State University, Mankato
Minnesota State University, Moorhead
Music Tech
Northwestern College†
Northwest Technical Institute School of CAD Technology
Oak Hills Christian College
Pine Technical College
Rasmussen College - Eagan*
Rasmussen College - Mankato*
Rasmussen College -Minnetonka*
Rasmussen College - St. Cloud*
Rochester Community & Technical College
St. John's University
St. Olaf College†
Sister Rosalind Gefre's Schools of Massage
Southwest State University*
University of Minnesota, Morris†
University of Minnesota - Twin Cities†
University of St. Thomas*
Winona State University

MISSOURI (3)
Stephens College†
Truman State University
Washington University of St. Louis

MONTANA (2/1)
Montana State University-Billings*
University of Montana

NEBRASKA (7)
Central Community College
Chadron State College
Grace University
Metropolitan Community College
Peru State College
Southeast Community College
Wayne State College

NEW HAMPSHIRE (11/3)
Colby-Sawyer College
Daniel Webster College
Dartmouth College†
Franklin Pierce College
Keene State College
New Hampshire College*
Notre Dame College*†
Plymouth State College†
Rivier College†
Saint Anselm College*†
University of New Hampshire

NEW JERSEY (3)
Fairleigh Dickinson University†
Saint Peter's College
Stevens Institute of Technology

NEW YORK (56/23)
Binghamton University
Broome Community College*
Canisius College*
Cayuga Community College*
Cazenovia College*
Clarkson University*†
Colgate University
(The) College of Saint Rose†
Daemen College
Elmira College†
Fashion Institute of Technology
Hamilton College
Hartwick College*†
Hobart and William Smith Colleges*
Hofstra University*
Houghton College*†
Keuka College†
Le Moyne College
Long Island University/C.W. Post Campus*
Manhattan College*
Marist College*
Mohawk Valley Community College
Nassau Community College
Nazareth College of Rochester*†

New York University
Niagara University*
Pace University
Paul Smith's College of Arts and Sciences
Plattsburgh State University of New York*
Rensselaer Polytechnic Institute†
Roberts Wesleyan College*
Rochester Institute of Technology†
St. John Fisher College*
St. John's University
St. Lawrence University
Sarah Lawrence College
School of Visual Arts*
Siena College
SUNY College at Brockport†
SUNY at Buffalo
SUNY College of Technology at Canton*
SUNY College of Agriculture & Tech. At Cobleskill
SUNY College at Cortland†
SUNY College of Technology at Delhi†
SUNY at Farmingdale
SUNY at New Paltz*
SUNY College at Oneonta
SUNY at Oswego
SUNY at Potsdam†
SUNY at Stony Brook†
Syracuse University†
Union College
University of Rochester
Utica College of Syracuse University*
Utica School of Commerce*
Wells College*

NORTH CAROLINA (2/0)
Gardner-Webb University
Lenoir-Rhyne College

NORTH DAKOTA (14/2)
Aakers Business College*
Bismarck State College
Dickinson State University
Jamestown College
Lake Region State College
Mayville State University†
Minot State University
Minot State University – Bottineau Campus
North Dakota State College of Science
North Dakota State University*
University of Mary
University of North Dakota
Valley City State University
Williston State College

OHIO (13/1)
Capital University
College of Mount St. Joseph
The College of Wooster
Denison University
John Carroll University
Lake Erie College
Marietta College
Mount Union College*
Muskingum College
Oberlin College
Ohio Wesleyan University
University of Dayton†
Xavier University†

OKLAHOMA (1)
The University of Tulsa
OREGON (4/2)
Concordia University*
George Fox University
Lewis & Clark College†
University of Portland*
PENNSYLVANIA (22/6)
Albright College
Allegheny College*
Arcadia University*†
Bradley Academy for the Visual Arts*
Carnegie Mellon University†
Cedar Crest College*
De Sales University
Elizabethtown College
Grove City College†
Gwynedd-Mercy College
Immaculata College
King's College*
Lehigh University

Moravian College
Robert Morris College
Seton Hill College
Temple University
Thiel College*
University of Pittsburgh†
U of the Sciences in Philadelphia
Washington & Jefferson College
York College of Pennsylvania†

RHODE ISLAND (11/2)
Brown University
Bryant College
Community College of Rhode Island
Johnson & Wales University*
New England Institute of Technology*
Providence College
Rhode Island College
Rhode Island School of Design
Roger Williams University
Salve Regina University
University of Rhode Island

SOUTH CAROLINA (2)
Columbia College
Presbyterian College†
SOUTH DAKOTA (3)
Augustana College
South Dakota State University
University of Sioux Falls

TENNESSEE (2/1)
Rhodes College*
Vanderbilt University†

TEXAS (2)
University of Dallas
University of the Incarnate Word

VERMONT (7/1)
Lyndon State College
Middlebury College
New England Culinary Institute
Norwich University
Saint Michael's College*
(The) University of Vermont†
Vermont Technical College

VIRGINIA (2)
Hollins University
University of Richmond†

WASHINGTON (18/4)
Centralia College
Central Washington University*
Eastern Washington University
Gonzaga University†
Heritage College*
Northwest College
Northwest Institute of Acupuncture & Oriental Medicine
Pacific Lutheran University*
Saint Martin's College*
Seattle University†
Spokane Falls Community College
University of Puget Sound†
University of Washington
Walla Walla College†
Washington State University
Western Washington University
Whitman College
Whitworth College†

WEST VIRGINIA (3/1)
College of West Virginia
West Liberty State College
Wheeling Jesuit University*

WISCONSIN (9/1)
Beloit College†
Carroll College
Edgewood College
Lakeshore Technical College
Lawrence University
Marian College of Fond du Lac
Marquette University
Ripon College*†
University of Wisconsin-Parkside

444 Total Collegiate Partners
120 Total Matching Partners
80 Total Collegiate Partners Plus
22 Total Matching Partners Plus
39 States Plus Washington D.C.

* Indicates participation in the Matching Partners program. Matching Partners agree to match Dollars for Scholars awards brought to their campuses.

† Indicates participation in the Partners Plus program. These part-ners go beyond the standard $1,000 agreement, allowing awards over $1,000 to replace students' unmet need or self-help.

APPENDIX E

ScholarShop Locations by Site (as of July, 2002)

ScholarShop Locations by State

All sites listed are ScholarShop (SS) sites unless otherwise noted.
JR = ScholarShop Jr., PS = ParentShop

Arizona
- Boys & Girls Club of Kayenta, Kayenta (SS, PS)

Arkansas
- Communities in Schools - Badgett Elementary, Little Rock (JR, PS only)
- The Harvey & Bernice Jones Center for Families, Springdale (SS, PS)

California
- Boys & Girls Club of Oakland, Oakland
- Boys & Girls Club of the Peninsula
  - –Herbert Hoover Branch, Menlo Park
  - –Mervin G. Morris Branch, Redwood City
- Boys & Girls Club of North San Mateo County, South San Francisco (SS, JR, PS)
- Community Youth Center, San Francisco
- Covenant House, Oakland
- YMCA of East Bay, Oakland
- MarVista Gardens Community Service Center, Culver City
- Mid-Peninsula Boys & Girls Club, San Mateo
- New Directions for Youth, Inc., Van Nuys (SS, JR, PS)
- Newark Memorial High School, Newark (SS, PS)
- San Diego Court & Community Schools, San Diego (SS, PS)
- Stuart M. Ketchum YMCA
  - –Central City Neighborhood Partners, Los Angeles (SS, PS)

Colorado
- Cheyenne Wells School, Cheyenne Wells
- Morgan County ScholarShop, Fort Morgan (JR only)

Connecticut
- WCSU Conn CAP/Upward Bound, Danbury, CT (SS, PS)
- Wesleyan Upward Bound, Middletown (SS, PS)

Georgia
- Beulah Enrichment & Resource Center, Decatur
- Boys & Girls Club of Metro Atlanta, Atlanta (SS, PS)
- Gainesville College PREP Program, Gainesville (SS, PS)
- Housing Authority of Fulton County, Atlanta (SS, PS)

Illinois

- Beardstown High School, Beardstown (SS, JR, PS)
- Chicago Assembly Plant Family Service & Learning Center, Chicago (SS, PS)
- Link & Option Center, South Holland (SS, PS)
- Lockport Community Education Foundation, Lockport
- North Lawndale Learning Community, Chicago (SS, JR, PS)
  - –Chalmers Elementary School
  - –Gregory Elementary School
  - –Dvorak Elementary School
  - –Johnson Elementary School
  - –Lathrop Elementary School
  - –Manley High School
- Northeastern Illinois University, Chicago - 9 Locations (SS, JR, PS)
- Southwest Youth Collaborative (SS, PS)
  - –Southwest Youth Collaborative, Chicago
  - –Arab American Action Network, Chicago
  - –Near North Youth Branch of SWYC, Chicago
- Winchester High School, Winchester

Indiana

- Boys & Girls Club of Indianapolis, Indianapolis - 5 Locations
- Boys & Girls Club of Tipton County, Tipton
- Marian College, Indianapolis (SS, PS)
  - –Scecina Memorial High School

Iowa

- Albia High School, Albia
- Davis County Schools
  - –Davis County High School, Bloomfield
  - –Davis County Middle School, Bloomfield
- Evans Middle School, Ottumwa
- Eddyville-Blakesburg Community Schools, Eddyville
- Jane Boyd Harambee House, Cedar Rapids
- Oskaloosa Community Schools, Oskaloosa
- West Branch Schools
  - –West Branch High School, West Branch (SS, PS)
  - –West Branch Middle School, West Branch (SS, PS)
- Woodrow Wilson Middle School, Sioux City (SS, PS)

Kansas

- Urban League of Wichita, Wichita

Kentucky

- Louisville Assembly Plant Family Service & Learning Center, Louisville (SS, PS)

Massachusetts

- YMCA of Greater Boston, Boston

248—Dr. Irving A. Fradkin

YMCA of Greater Worcester - Central Branch, Worcester

<u>Michigan</u>

Milan Plastics Plant Family Services & Learning Center, Milan (SS, PS)
Monroe High School, Monroe
Rawsonville Family Services & Learning Center, Rawsonville (SS, PS)
Sterling Plant Family Services & Learning Center, Sterling Heights (SS, PS)
Ypsilanti Family Services & Learning Center, Ypsilanti (SS, PS)

<u>Minnesota</u>

Boys & Girls Club of Elk River - Lion's Park Unit, Elk River (SS, JR, PS)
Concordia College, Moorhead (JR, PS ONLY)
Elmore Academy ScholarShop, Elmore
–YSI
–Elmore Academy
Higher Ground Academy, St Paul, MN (SS, PS)
Life Skills Development Center, St. Paul (SS, JR, PS)
North Intermediate School, St. Peter (JR, PS ONLY)
St. Peter Community ScholarShop, St. Peter (SS, JR, PS)
Twin Cities Boys & Girls Club - Jerry Gamble Branch, Minneapolis
Urban Ventures, Minneapolis (SS, PS)

<u>Nebraska</u>

Bertrand Community Schools, Bertrand

Nevada

Boys & Girls of Club of Las Vegas, Las Vegas (SS, PS)

<u>New Jersey</u>

Rutgers University – CSUC, Camden (SS, JR, PS)

<u>New York</u>

The Bob Lanier Center LPP, Buffalo (SS, JR, PS)
Binghamton University LPP, Binghamton (SS, JR, PS)
–SUNY Morrisville, Norwich
Bronx Community College, Bronx (SS, PS)
Buffalo Stamping Plant, Buffalo (SS, PS)
College of Staten Island LPP, Staten Island (SS, JR, PS)
–College of Staten Island
–Intermediate School District #49
–Wagner High School
–Curtis High School
–New Dorp High School
Genesee Community College, Albion (SS, PS)
Hostos Community College, Hostos (SS, PS)
LaGuardia Community College LPP, Long Island (SS, PS)
–Saturday Center @ LaGuardia Community College
–Newton High School

–Grover Cleveland High School
–Franklin K Lane High School
–International Charter High School
Marist College LPP, Poughkeepsie
–Poughkeepsie Middle School, Poughkeepsie (SS, JR, PS)
–Poughkeepsie High School, Poughkeepsie (SS, PS)
–Gov. George Clinton School, Poughkeepsie (JR, PS Only)
–Warring Academy, Poughkeepsie (JR, PS Only)
–Miller Middle School, Lake Katrine (SS, JR, PS)
–Bailey Middle School, Kingston (SS, PS)
–Kingston High School, Kingston (SS, PS)
Metro Center NYU, New York, NY (SS, PS)
Monroe Community College LPP, Rochester (SS, PS)
Nassau community college LPP, Garden City (SS, PS)
New York City Consortium (SS, PS)
–John Jay College LPP, New York
–PACE University LPP, New York
–Barnard College LPP, New York
–Medgar Evers College LPP, Brooklyn
–Kingsborough Community College LPP, Brooklyn
Orange County Community College LPP, Newburgh (SS, JR, PS)
Puerto Rican Youth Development LPP, Rochester
Queensborough Community College LPP, Bayside (SS, PS)
Roosevelt High School, Yonkers (SS, JR, PS)
SUC at Rockland LPP, Suffern - 4 Libraries (SS, PS)
SUC at Purchase LPP, Purchase (SS, PS)
Suffolk County Community College LPP, Selden (SS, PS)
SUNY Albany LPP, Albany (SS, JR, PS)
SUNY at Canton, Canton (SS, PS)
SUNY at Stony Brook LPP, Stony Brook
–Brentwood High School (SS, PS)
Syracuse University School Consortium LPP, Syracuse - 2 Libraries (SS, JR, PS)
–Onondaga Community College
–Corcoran High School
–Fowler High School
–Syracuse University - 3 Libraries
–Le Moyne College
–Henninger High School
–Nottingham High School
Urban League of Long Island LPP, Central Islip
Utica College LPP, Utica (SS, PS)
–Thomas R. Proctor High School, Utica
–James H. Donovan Middle School, Utica
–John F. Kennedy Middle School, Utica
Western New York LPP Consortium (SS, PS)
–Daemen College, Amherst
–SUC at Buffalo, Buffalo

–SUC at Fredonia, Fredonia
–SUNY Buffalo, Buffalo
–Canisius College, Buffalo

North Carolina
Raleigh Boys & Girls Club - Teen Center, Raleigh

North Dakota
Lakota High School, Lakota (SS, JR, PS)

Ohio
Lima Engine Plant Family Service & Learning Center, Lima (SS, PS)
Sandusky Plastics Plant Family Services & Learning Center (SS, PS)

Oklahoma
Texas County Extention, Guymon
Tulsa Glass Plant Family Services & Learning Center (SS, PS)

Pennsylvania
Arcadia University, Glenside(SS, JR, PS)
–Imhotep Institute Charter High School
–Communiversity @ Imhotep
–Imani Education Circle Elementary Charter School
–Harambee Institute Charter School
Glenwood YMCA, Erie (SS, PS)
McKeesport YMCA, McKeesport (SS, PS)

Texas
Boysville, Converse
McLennan County Youth Collaboration, Waco
PATCH Counseling Center, Port Neches
St. Martin DePorres Church, Crosby

Washington
Sumner Schools, Sumner

Washington D.C
US Dream Academy (SS, PS)

Wisconsin
Madison Housing Community
–Northport Community Learning Center, Madison (SS, JR, PS)
–Packer Community Learning Center, Madison (SS, JR, PS)

In addition to the sites listed above, ParentShop is used at over 80 locations throughout the nation.